AGGRESSIVE CHRISTIANITY.

MARK xvi. 15.—*" Go ye into all the world and preach the Gospel to every creature."*

ACTS xxvi. 15-18.—*" And I said, Who art thou, Lord? And he said, I am Jesus whom thou persecutest But rise, and stand upon thy feet · for I have appeared unto thee for this purpose, to make thee a minister and a witness both of these things which thou hast seen, and of those things in the which I will appear unto thee: Delivering thee from the people, and from the Gentiles, unto whom now I send thee, to open their eyes, and to turn them from darkness to light, and from the power of Satan unto God, that they may receive forgiveness of sins, and inheritance among them which are sanctified by faith that is in me."*

I WAS thinking, while I was reading the lesson, that, supposing we could blot out from our minds all knowledge of the history of Christianity from the time of this Inauguration Service—from that Pentecostal Baptism—or, at any rate, from the close of the period described in the Acts of the Apostles, suppose we could detach from our minds all knowledge of the history of Christianity since then, and take the Acts of the Apostles and sit down and calculate what was likely to happen in the world, what different results we should have anticipated, what a different world we should have reckoned upon as the outcome of it all. A system which commenced under such auspices, with such assumptions and professions on the part of its Author (speaking after the manner of men), and producing, as it did, in the first century of its existence, such

gigantic and momentous results. We should have said,
if we knew nothing of what has intervened from that
time to this, that, no doubt, the world where that war
commenced, and for which it was organised, would have
long since been subjugated to the influence of that
system, and brought under the power of its great
originator and founder! I say, from reading these
Acts, and from observing the spirit which animated the
early disciples, and from the way in which everything
fell before them, we should have anticipated that ten
thousand times greater results would have followed,
and, in my judgment, this anticipation would have
been perfectly rational and just.

We Christians profess to possess in the Gospel of
Christ a mighty lever which, rightly and universally
applied, would lift the entire burden of sin and misery
from the shoulders, that is, from the souls, of our
fellow-men—a panacea, we believe it to be, for all the
moral and spiritual woes of humanity, and in curing
their spiritual plagues we should go far to cure their
physical plagues also. We all profess to believe this.
Christians have professed to believe this for generations
gone by, ever since the time of which we have been
reading, and yet look at the world, look at so-called
Christian England, in this end of the nineteenth
century! The great majority of the nation utterly
ignoring God, and not even making any pretence of
remembering Him one day in the week. And then
look at the rest of the world. I have frequently got so
depressed with this view of things that I have felt as
if my heart would break. I don't know how other
Christians feel, but I can truly say that "rivers of
water do often run down my eyes because men keep

Papers on Aggressive Christianity

Catherine Mumford Booth

BIBLIOLIFE

PAPERS

ON

AGGRESSIVE CHRISTIANITY.

BY

MRS. BOOTH.

London:

INTERNATIONAL HEADQUARTERS: 101, QUEEN VICTORIA ST., E.C
PRINTING & PUBLISHING OFFICES·
98, 100, & 102, CLERKENWELL ROAD, E.C.
JOHN SNOW & CO., 2, IVY LANE, PATERNOSTER ROW, E.C.
AND BY ORDER OF ANY BOOKSELLER.

1891.

PREFACE.

THE addresses contained in this little volume were delivered during a series of services at the West End of London, in the summer of 1880. That they were used then of the Lord I had abundant evidence, and on that account I have consented to their reproduction in this form, hoping that He may still speak through them to many souls.

I only regret that pressing public duties have prevented the shorthand writer's notes being revised as thoroughly as I could have wished, especially as they are reports of what were themselves largely unpremeditated utterances.

CATHERINE BOOTH.

London, December, 1880.

CONTENTS.

AGGRESSIVE CHRISTIANITY.

not His law," and because it seems to me that this dispensation, compared with what God intended it to be, has been, and still is, as great a failure as that which preceded it.

Now, I ask, how is this? I do not for a moment believe that this is in accordance with the purpose of God. Some people have a very convenient way of hiding behind God's purposes, and saying, 'Oh! He will do His own will.' I wish He did! They say, 'You know God's will is done after all.' I wish it were! *He* says it is *not* done, and over and over again laments the fact that it is not done. He wants it to be done, but it is NOT DONE! 'It is of no use to stand up and propound theories that are at variance with things as they are.' There has been a great deal too much of this, and it has had a very bad effect. The world is in this condition, and here is a system launched under such auspices, with such purposes, with such promises, and with such prospects, and yet nearly nineteen hundred years have rolled away and here we are. How little has been done, comparatively. What a little alteration has been effected in the habits and dispositions of the race.

But some of you will say, 'Well, but there is a good deal done.' Thank God for that. It would be sad if there were *nothing* done; but it looks like a drop in the ocean compared with what should have been done. Now I cannot accept any theory which so far reflects upon the love and goodness of God as to make *Him* to blame for this effeteness of Christianity, and, so far as my influence extends, I will not allow the responsibility and the blame of all this to be rolled back upon God. who so loved the world that He gave

His only Son to ignominy and death in order to
redeem it.   I do not believe it for a moment.   I
believe that the old arch-enemy has done in this
dispensation what he did in former ones—so far
circumvented the purposes of God, that he has
succeeded in bringing about this state of things—in
retarding the accomplishment of God's purposes and
keeping the world thus largely under his own power
and influence, and I believe he has succeeded in doing
this, as he has succeeded always before, by DECEIVING
GOD'S OWN PEOPLE.   He has always done so.   He has
always got up a caricature of God's real thing, and
the nearer he can get it to be like the original the
more successful he is.   He has succeeded in deceiving
God's people :—

First :—AS TO THE STANDARD OF THEIR OWN RELIGIOUS
LIFE.

And, *Secondly,* he has succeeded in deceiving them
AS TO THEIR DUTIES AND OBLIGATIONS TO THE WORLD.

He has succeeded, first, in deceiving them as to the
standard of their own religious life.   He has got the
Church, nearly as a whole, to receive what I call an
' Oh, wretched man that I am' religion!   He has got
them to lower the standard which Jesus Christ himself
established in this Book—a standard, not only to be
aimed at, but to be attained unto—a standard of
victory over sin, the world, the flesh, and the Devil,
real, living, reigning, triumphing, Christianity!
Satan knew what was the secret of the great success
of those early disciples.   It was their whole-hearted
devotion, their absorbing love to Christ, their utter
abnegation of the world.   It was their entire absorption
in the salvation of their fellow men and the glory of

their God. It was an enthusiastic religion that swallowed them up, and made them willing to become wanderers and vagabonds on the face of the earth—for His sake to dwell in dens and caves, to be torn asunder, and to be persecuted in every form.

It was this degree of devotion, before which Satan saw he had no chance. Such people as these, he knew, must ultimately subdue the world. It is not in human nature to stand before that kind of spirit, that amount of love and zeal, and if Christians had only gone on as they began long since, the glorious prophecy would have been fulfilled, " The kingdoms of this world" would have " become the kingdoms of our Lord and of his Christ."

Therefore, the arch-enemy said, ' What must I do? ' I shall be defeated after all. I shall lose my ' supremacy as the god of this world. What shall I ' do?' No use to bring in a gigantic system of error, which everybody will see to be error. Oh, dear no! That has never been Satan's way; but his plan has been to get hold of a good man here and there, who shall creep in, as the Apostle said, unawares, and preach another doctrine, and who shall deceive, if it were possible, the very elect. *And he did it.* He accomplished his design. He gradually lowered the standard of Christian life and character, and though, in every revival, God has raised it again to a certain extent, we have never got back thoroughly to the simplicity, purity, and devotion set before us in these Acts of the Apostles and in the Epistles. And just in the degree that it has approximated thereto, in every age, Satan has got somebody to oppose and to show that this was too high a standard for human nature, altogether beyond us, and that, therefore, Christians must sit down and just be content to be " Oh wretched man that I am " people to the end of their days. He has got the Church into a condition that makes one, sometimes, positively ashamed to hear professing Christians talk, and ashamed also, that the world should hear them talk. I do not wonder at thoughtful, intelligent men being driven from such Christianity as this. It would have driven me off, if I had not known the *power* of godliness. I believe this kind of Christianity has made more infidels than all the infidel books ever written.

Yes, Satan knew that he must get Christians down from the high pinnacle of whole-hearted consecration to God. He knew that he had no chance till he tempted them down from that blessed vantage ground, and so he began to spread those false doctrines, to counteract which John wrote his epistles, for, before he died, he saw what was coming, and sounded down the ages—" Little children, let no man deceive you : he that doeth righteousness is righteous, even as He is righteous. He that committeth sin is of the devil ; for the devil sinneth from the beginning. For this purpose the Son of God was manifested, that He might destroy the works of the devil." The Lord revive that doctrine ! Help us afresh to put up the standard !

Oh ! the great evil is, that dishonest-hearted people, because they feel it condemns them, lower the standard to their miserable experience. I said, when I was young, and I repeat it in my maturer years, that if it sent me to hell I would never pull it down. Oh ! that God's people felt like that There is the glorious standard put before us. The power is proffered, the conditions laid down, and we CAN all attain it if we will; but if we will not—for the sake of the children, and for generations yet unborn, do not let us drag it down, and try to make it meet our little, paltry, circumscribed experience. LET US KEEP IT UP. This is the way to get the world to look at it. Show the world a real, living, self-sacrificing, hard-working, toiling, triumphing religion, and the world will be influenced by it; but anything short of that they will turn round and spit upon.

Secondly :—Satan has deceived even those whom he could not succeed in getting to lower the standard of their own lives with respect to their duties and obligations to the world. I have been reading of late the New Testament with special reference to the aggressive spirit of Primitive Christianity, and it is wonderful what floods of light come upon you when you read the Bible with reference to any particular topic on which you are seeking for help. When God sees you are panting after the light, in order that you may use it, *He pours it in upon you.* It is an indispensable condition of receiving light that you are willing to follow it. People say they don't see this and that, no, because they do not wish to see. They are not willing to walk in it, and, therefore, they do not get it; but those who are willing to obey shall have all the light they want.

It seems to me that we come infinitely short of any right and rational idea of the aggressive spirit of the New Testament saints. Satan has got Christians to accept what I may call a namby-pamby, kid-glove kind of system of presenting the Gospel to people.

2

'Will they be so kind as to read this tract or book, or
'would they not like to hear this popular and eloquent
'preacher.   They will be pleased with him quite apart
'from religion.'   That is the sort of half-frightened,
timid way of putting the truth before unconverted
people, and of talking to them about the salvation of
their souls.   It seems to me this is utterly antagonistic
and repugnant to the spirit of the early saints : " Go
ye, and preach the Gospel to EVERY CREATURE ;"
and again the same idea—" Unto whom now I send
thee."   Look what is implied in these commissions.
It seems to me that no people have ever yet fathomed
the meaning of these two Divine commissions.   I
believe we of the Salvation Army have come nearer to
it than any people that have ever preceded us.   Look
at them.   Would it ever occur to you that the
language meant, " Go and build chapels and churches
" and invite the people to come in, and if they will
" not, let them alone ? "   " GO YE."   If you sent your
servant to do something for you, and said, ' Go and
accomplish that piece of business for me.'   You know
what it would involve.   You know that he must see
certain persons ; and run about the city to certain offices
and banks and agents, involving a deal of trouble and
sacrifice ; but you have nothing to do with that.   He
is *your servant.*   He is employed by you to do that
business, and you simply commission him to ' Go and
do it.'   What would you think if he went and took an
office and sent out a number of circulars inviting your
customers or clients to come and wait on his pleasure,
and when they chose to come just to put your business
before them ?   No, you would say, ' Ridiculous.'
Divesting our minds of all conventionalities and

traditionalisms, what would the language mean? "Go ye!" To whom? "To every creature." Where am I to get at them? WHERE THEY ARE. "Every creature." There is the extent of your commission. Seek them out; run after them, where-ever you can get at them. "Every creature"— wherever you find a creature that has a soul—there go and preach My Gospel to him. If I understand it, *that* is the meaning and the spirit of the commission.

And then again, to Paul he says, "Unto whom now I send thee, to open their eyes, *and* to turn *them* from darkness to light, and *from* the power of Satan unto God." They are asleep—go and wake them up. They do not see their danger. If they did, there would be no necessity for you to run after them. They are *preoccupied.* Open their eyes, and turn them round by your desperate earnestness and moral suasion and moral force; oh! it makes me tremble to think what a great deal one man can do for another! "Turn them from darkness to light, and from the power of Satan unto God." How did Paul understand it? He says, "We persuade men." Do not rest content with just putting it before them, giving them gentle invitations, and then leaving them alone. He ran after them, poor things, and pulled them out of the fire. Take the bandage off their eyes which Satan has bound round them; knock and hammer and burn in, with the fire of the Holy Ghost, your words into their poor, hardened, darkened hearts, until they begin to realise that they are IN DANGER; that there is something amiss. Go after them. If I understand it, that is the spirit of the Apostles and of the early Christians; for we read that when they were scattered by persecution, they " went *everywhere,* preaching the word." The laity, the new converts, the young babes in Christ. It does not mean always in set discourses, and public assemblies, but they went after men and women, like ancient Israel—" Every man after his man," to try and win him for Christ.

Some people seem to think that the Apostles laid the foundations of all the churches. They are quite mistaken. Churches sprang up where the Apostles had never been. The Apostles went to visit and organise them after they had sprung up, as the result of the work of the early laymen and women going everywhere and preaching the Word. Oh! may the Lord shower upon us in this day the same spirit! We should build churches and chapels; we should invite the people to them; but do you think it is consistent with these two commissions, and with many others, that we should rest in this, when three parts of the population utterly ignore our invitations and take no notice whatever of our buildings and of our services? *They will not come to us.* That is an established fact. What is to be done? They have souls. You profess to believe that as much as I do, and that they must live for ever. Where are they going? What is to be done? Jesus Christ says, 'Go after them.' When all the civil methods have failed; when the genteel invitations have failed; when one man says that he has married a wife, and another that he has bought a yoke of oxen, and another that he has bought a piece of land—then does the Master of the feast say, ' The ungrateful wretches, let them alone ? ' " No." He says, " Go out into the highways and hedges, and compel them to come in, that my house may be filled." I will have guests, and if you can't get them in by civil measures, use military measures. Go and COMPEL them to come in. It seems to me that we want more of this determined aggressive spirit. Those of you who are right with God this afternoon—you want more of this spirit to thrust the truth upon the attention of your fellow men.

Oh! people say, you must be very careful, very judicious. You must not thrust religion down people's throats. Then, I say, you will never get it down. What! Am I to wait till an unconverted, godless man *wants* to be saved before I try to save him? He will never want to be saved till the death-rattle is in his throat. What! Am I to let my unconverted friends and acquaintances drift down quietly to damnation, and never tell them about their souls, until they say, 'If you please, I want you to preach to me?' Is this anything like the spirit of early Christianity? No. Verily we must *make* them look—tear the bandages off, open their eyes, make them bear it, and if they run away from you in one place, meet them in another, and let them have no peace until they submit to God and get their souls saved. This is what Christianity *ought* to be doing in this land, and there are plenty of Christians to do it. Why, we might give the world such a time of it that they would get saved in very *self defence,* if we were only up and doing, and determined that they should have no peace in their sins. Where is our zeal for the Lord? We talk of Old Testament saints, but I would we were all like David. Rivers of water ran down his eyes because men kept not the Law of his God. But you say, 'We cannot all hold services.' Perhaps not.

Go as you like. Go as quietly and softly as the morning dew. Have meetings like the Friends if you like. ONLY DO IT. Don't let your relatives, and friends, and acquaintances die, and their blood be found on your skirts ! ! !

I shall never forget the agony depicted on the face of a young lady who once came to see me. My heart went out to her in pity. She told me her story. She said, 'I had a proud, ungodly father, and the Lord 'converted me three years before his death, and, from 'the very day of my conversion, I felt I ought to 'talk to him, and plead, and pray with him about 'his soul, but I could not muster up courage. I 'kept intending to do it, and intending to do it, 'until he was taken ill. It was a sudden and serious 'illness. He lost his mind, and died unsaved,' and she said, 'I have never smiled since, and I think I 'never shall any more.' Don't be like that. Do it quietly, if you like; privately, if you like; but do it, and do it as if you felt the value of their souls, and as if you intended to save them, if by any possible means in your power it could be done.

I had been speaking in a town, in the West of England, on the subject of *responsibility* of Christians for the salvation of souls. The gentlemen with whom I was staying had winced a bit under the truth, and instead of taking it to heart in love, and making it the means of drawing him nearer to God, and enabling him to serve Him better, he said, ' I thought you were 'rather hard on us this morning.' I said, 'Did you? ' I should be very sorry to be harder on anybody than 'the Lord Jesus Christ would be.' He said, 'You 'can push things to extremes, you know. You were

' talking about seeking souls, and making sacrifices.
' Now, you are aware that we build the chapels and
' churches, and pay the ministers, and if the people
' won't be saved, we can't help it.' (I think he had
given pretty largely to a chapel in the town.) I said,
' It is very heartless and ungrateful of the people, I
' grant; but, my dear sir, you would not reason thus
' in any temporal matter. Suppose a plague were to
' break out in London, and suppose that the Board of
' Health were to meet and to appropriate all the
' hospitals and public buildings they could get to the
' treatment of those diseased, and suppose they were
' to issue proclamations to say that whoever would
' come to these buildings should be treated free of
' cost, and every care and kindness bestowed on them,
' and, moreover, that the treatment would certainly
' cure them ; but, supposing the people were so blind
' to their own interests, so indifferent and besotted
' that they refused to come, and consequently, the
' plague was increasing and thousands dying, what
' would you in the provinces say ? Would you say,
' " Well, the Board of Health have done what they
' " could, and if the people will not go to be healed,
' " they deserve to perish ; let them alone ?' No, you
' would say, ' It is certainly very foolish and wicked of
' " the people, but these men are in a superior position.
' " They understand the matter. They know and are
' " responsible for the consequences. What in the
' " world are they going to do ? Let the whole land be
' " depopulated !' No! If the people will not come
' to them, they must go to the people, and force upon
' them the means of health, and insist that proper
' measures should be used for the suppression of the

'plague.' It needed no application. He understood
it, and I believe, by the Spirit of God, he was enabled
to see his mistake, to take it home, and set to work to
do something for perishing souls.

Men are preoccupied, and it is for us to go and
force it upon their attention. Remember, you can do
it. There is some *one soul* that you have more
influence with than any other person on earth—some
soul or souls. Are you doing all you can for their
salvation? Your relatives, friends, and acquaintances
are to be rescued. Thank God! we are rescuing the
poor people all over the land by thousands. There
they are, to be looked at, and talked with, and
questioned—people rescued from the depths of sin,
degradation, and woe—saved from the worst forms of
crime and infamy; and, if He can do that, He can
save your genteel friends, if only you will go to them
desperately and determinedly. Take them lovingly
by the button-hole, and say, 'My dear friend, I never
'spoke to you closely, carefully, and prayerfully about
'your soul.' Let them see the tears in your eyes; or,
if you cannot weep, let them *hear the tears in your
voice*, and let them realise that you feel their danger,
and are in distress for them. God will give His Holy
Spirit, and they *will be saved.*

I was going to note that both texts imply opposition
—for, He adds, "Lo, I am with you always, even to
the end of the world." As much as if He had said,
'You will have need of my presence. Such aggressive,
'determined warfare as this will raise all earth and
'hell against you;' and then He says to Paul, "I will
be with thee, delivering thee from the people and the
Gentiles unto whom I send thee." Why would they

need this? Because the Gentiles would soon be up in arms against him, and indeed they were.

Opposition! It is a bad sign for the Christianity of this day that it provokes so little opposition. If there were no other evidence of it being wrong, I should know it from that. When the Church and the world can jog along comfortably together, you may be sure there is something wrong. The world has not altered. Its spirit is exactly the same as it ever was, and if Christians were equally faithful and devoted to the Lord, and separated from the world, living so that their lives were a reproof to all ungodliness, the world would hate them as much as ever it did. It is the *Church* that has altered, *not* the world. You say, 'We should be getting into endless turmoil.' Yes; "I came not to bring peace on the earth, but a sword." There would be uproar. Yes; and the Acts of the Apostles are full of stories of uproars. One uproar was so great that the Chief Captain had to get Paul over the shoulders of the people, lest he should have been torn in pieces. 'What a commotion!' you say. Yes; and, bless God, if we had the like now we should have thousands of sinners saved.

'But,' you say, 'see what a very undignified position this would bring the Gospel into.' That depends on what sort of dignity you mean. You say, 'We should always be getting into collision with the powers that be, and with the world, and what very unpleasant consequences would result.' Yes, dear friends, there always have been unpleasant consequences to the flesh, when people were following God and doing His will. 'But,' you say, 'wouldn't it be inconsistent with the dignity of the Gospel.' It depends from what stand-

point you look at it.   It depends upon what really
constitutes the dignity of the Gospel. What does
constitute the dignity of the Gospel?   Is it human
dignity, or is it Divine?   Is it earthly, or is it heavenly
dignity?   It was a very undignified thing, looked at
humanly, to die on a cross between two thieves.   That
was the most undignified thing ever done in this world,
and yet, looked at on moral and spiritual grounds, it
was the grandest spectacle that ever earth or heaven
gazed upon, and methinks that the inhabitants of
heaven stood still and looked over the battlements at
that glorious, illustrious sufferer, as He hung there
between heaven and earth.   The Pharisees, I know,
spat upon the humbled sufferer, and wagged their
heads and said, " He saved others, himself He cannot
save." Ah! but He was intent on saving others.   That
was the dignity of Almighty strength allying itself
with human weakness, in order to raise it.   It was the
dignity of eternal wisdom shrouding itself in human
ignorance, in order to enlighten it.   It was the
dignity of everlasting, unquenchable love, baring its
bosom to suffer in the stead of its rebellious creature
—man.   Ah! it was incarnate God standing in the
place of condemned, apostate man—the dignity of love!
love! Love!

Oh, precious Saviour! save us from maligning Thy
Gospel and Thy name by clothing it with our paltry
notions of earthly dignity, and forgetting the dignity
which crowned Thy sacred brow as Thou didst hang
upon the cross!   That is the dignity for us, and it will
never suffer by any gentleman here carrying the Gospel
into the back slums or alleys of any town or city in
which he lives.   That dignity will never suffer by any

employer talking lovingly to his servant maid or errand boy, and looking into his eyes with tears of sympathy and love and trying to bring his soul to Jesus. That dignity will never suffer even though you should have to be dragged through the streets with a howling mob at your heels, like Jesus Christ, if you have gone into those streets for the souls of your fellow men and the glory of God. Though you should be tied to a stake, as were the martyrs of old, and surrounded by laughing and taunting fiends and their howling followers—that will be a dignity which shall be crowned in heaven, crowned with everlasting glory. If I understand it, *that* is the dignity of the Gospel—the dignity of love. I do not envy, I do not covet any other. I desire no other, —God is my witness—than the dignity of love.

Oh, friends! will you get this baptism of love! Then you will, like the Apostles, be willing to push your limbs into a basket, and so be let down by the wall, if need be, or suffer shipwreck, hunger, peril, nakedness, fire, or sword, or even go to the block itself, if thereby you may extend His kingdom and win souls for whom He shed His blood. The Lord fill us with this love and baptise us with this fire, and then the Gospel will arise and become glorious in the earth, and men will believe in us, and in it. They will feel its power, and they will go down under it by thousands, and, by the grace of God, they SHALL.

A PURE GOSPEL.

A PURE GOSPEL.

Acts xxvi. 15-20 —"*And I said, Who art thou, Lord? And he
said, I am Jesus whom thou persecutest But rise, and stand
upon thy feet. for I have appeared unto thee for this purpose,
to make thee a minister and a witness both of these things
which thou hast seen, and of those things in the which I will
appear unto thee delivering thee from the people, and from
the Gentiles, unto whom now I send thee, to open their eyes,
and to turn them from darkness to light, and from the power
of Satan unto God, that they may receive forgiveness of sins,
and inheritance among them which are sanctified by faith that
is in me. Whereupon, O king Agrippa, I was not disobedient
unto the heavenly vision · but shewed first unto them of
Damascus, and at Jerusalem, and throughout all the coasts
of Judea, and then to the Gentiles, that they should repent
and turn to God, and do works meet for repentance.*"

THE *second* indispensable condition we are going to
note this afternoon, to Aggressive Christianity, is, a
Pure Gospel. I mean by that, God's own pure metal
— the unadulterated Gospel of Jesus Christ.

There seems, now-a-days, in the Church and the
world, as many different views of the Gospel as there
are of secondary matters and of minor doctrines. One
person has one notion of the Gospel, another has
another, until there has come to be a fearful dis-
traction in the minds of many who are constantly
listening to what is called the Gospel. May God
the Holy Ghost help us this afternoon to look at it
impartially and carefully.

And, *firstly*, let me try to define *what is the Gospel.*
" Oh ! " people say, " it is good news." Yes, thank

God, it is good news, indeed—news without which
we must all have been lost.   It is the news of the
free, measureless, undeserved, reconciling mercy of
God, offered to me through the vicarious, infinite,
glorious sacrifice of His Son, to the end that I may
BE SAVED from sin here and from hell hereafter !!
But this news involves a great deal.   It is the news
of a definite, practical end, involving conditions ; for
even good news to me involves certain conditions on
my part, if I am to procure the good which the news
brings.   Then, *secondly*, I will try to explain the
conditions on which the Gospel is available to me.

Let me illustrate this; and I am particularly anxious
that you should all understand me.   Supposing that
a province of this empire were in rebellion against
our Sovereign.   Supposing that the people of that
province had trampled under foot our laws, and set
up their own in opposition ; and suppose the Queen,
in her gracious clemency, desired not to destroy these
rebels, but to save them, what would be the necessary
and indispensable condition in the very nature of the
case, in order for her to save them ?   Not merely a
proclamation of pardon.   That would be a glorious
movement towards the result, but there would want
something else ; for a proclamation of pardon merely,
whilst the rebels remained in an unchanged state,
would only be giving them greater facilities for
further rebellion.   Evidently, in the nature of the
case, it is a necessity that a change of mind should
be produced in the rebels themselves, for the Queen
not only wants to save them from destruction, but
to restore them to allegiance and obedience to herself, and, unless she does this, they will never become

dutiful and obedient subjects. There will never be anything but anarchy, confusion, and rebellion in that province unless those rebels undergo a change of mind. They must be brought back to allegiance and obedience to the Queen.

Just so with God's proclamation of salvation. The mischief is in us. Take the illustration of the Prodigal Son. The mischief was all in him—not in his father. The father loved him before he went away, and the father loved him afterwards. The father's benevolent heart yearned over him all the time he was away, and many a time, perchance, he went to the roof of his house to look over the expanse of country over which the rebellious lad had gone and wondered whether he would ever come back. The father's heart was yearning over him all the time. How was it that he could not be reinstated in the father's love and in the family privileges ? Because there needed a change of heart—a change of mind in HIM. If he had come back to the old homestead with the same rebellious spirit in him, the same desire to be free from the father's oversight, the same unwillingness to be put under the FATHER'S DOMINION and DISCIPLINE, he would still have been a rebel and a prodigal. In the very nature of the case, until there was the necessary change, a wise and righteous father could not pardon him; he must insist, though he loves him dearly, upon a certain change of mind before he can consistently pardon him.

Just so. The laws of mind are the same when operated upon by either God or man. This is not laying any necessity upon God any more than He has laid upon Himself. He has made us with a

3

certain mental constitution, and therefore He must
adapt the conditions and means of our salvation to
that mental constitution, otherwise He would reflect
upon His own wisdom in having given it to us at the
first.   Therefore when he purposes to save man He
must save him *as man*—not as a beast or a machine!
He must save him as man, and he must propound
such a scheme as will fit and adapt itself to man's
nature.   Just as the father might not pardon the
prodigal, irrespective of the prodigal's state of mind
and heart, so neither can God pardon the sinner
irrespective of the state of his mind and heart.

I know, by personal contact with hundreds of souls,
that there is an alarming amount of misunderstanding
and of what I consider false apprehension of the Gospel
of Christ at this point.   Hence, you have speakers
saying, without anything to guard or qualify their
words, 'Only believe, and you shall be saved;'
'Whosoever believeth hath everlasting life.'   Blessed
and glorious truth, *when rightly applied, and applied
to the right characters;* but dangerous error, in my
opinion, *when applied indiscriminately to unawakened
unrepenting, rebellious sinners.*   I have met with
disastrous consequences of this all over the land—so
disastrous that I would not like to repeat them here.
Now, I say, we should be careful to let the people
understand what we mean by the Gospel : I dare not
do any other.   I am so satisfied of the thousands of
souls that are deceived at this point, that, while God
gives me voice to speak, I dare not but try to warn
them, and show them their fatal mistake.

Returning to our illustration—you say, 'The man
is, so to speak, dead in trespasses and sins.   How can

he see his own error? How can he lay down the weapons of rebellion? How can he, by himself, come back to the Father?' Granted. Hence, God, in His wisdom and love, has provided for that incapacity which man has induced by his rebellion, by the gift of His Spirit. You say, 'The parallel is not perfect between your illustration and the thing illustrated.' No, it is not in that point; because temporal rebels can find out by themselves the insanity and wickedness of their course. They can see where it will lead them. They can see the destructive consequences, and be sorry for the course they have taken. They can lay down their weapons of rebellion, and they can conform to the conditions on which the Queen issues her proclamation. You say, 'Yes, *that* they can do, but *this* man cannot.' Of course, because he has so hardened his heart that even if he *can*, he never *will* without the Holy Spirit of God. Hence, God has taken compassion on us, and sent His Spirit into the world for this purpose—'To convince the world of sin, of righteousness, and of judgment.' Thus He opens our eyes, and shows us our lost estate. Having, by the Holy Ghost, made us realise our desperate condition, then comes the Gospel to meet us just where we are, on condition that we abandon our evil ways, and do the works meet for repentance, which we are *able to do* by the power of the Holy Spirit, as well as to lay down the weapons of our rebellion and accept of Christ, put our neck under his yoke, and pledge ourselves in heart to FOLLOW HIM ALL THE DAYS OF OUR LIFE. These are the conditions involved, and this is the end the Gospel contemplates, and there you see the Gospel accomplishes its END in this case. The heart of the rebel is won back to its Lord, and the indispensable change has taken place in the *being himself*. He has come back to God. His eyes are opened to see the evil of sin, and the desperate state he is in. Tired of himself, and tired of his evil ways, as the Prodigal was of the swine-yard, he arises, leaves them and goes to his father.

But now I must stop to meet a difficulty which I know will arise in many sincere minds. I feel myself such a tender jealousy for the glory of God, that I do highly respect this feeling in others, and if anyone disagrees with my views, or my way of putting them, through a feeling of jealousy for the glory of God, they have my profound respect. You will say, " If we are able to abandon our evil courses, and lay down the weapons of rebellion, is that not saving ourselves?' No, dear friends; it is altogether different. You see it is the indispensable condition of salvation in everyone of the nine passages we read, and in many others—that we abandon our evil ways. Now, what does that mean ? A gentleman in a letter to me said, ' We cannot save ourselves from heart sins.' Granted ; but we can *will* to be saved from them. Then, there is a great distinction between those sins of the heart, which are involuntary, and those deliberate transgressions of God's law, which unregenerate men commit. God requires me to abandon all that I CAN, as a condition of salvation, and then, when He saves, He will give me power to abandon all that I could; not before. The Prodigal had to come away from the swine-yard, the filth, and the husks, before he got into the father's house, and sat down at the fathers feast, but when he had done so, then the father said, ' Come in,' and he brought the best robe and put it on him, and killed the fatted calf, and put the ring of forgiveness upon his hand. Hence, as the old divines used to put it, "You must wait for the Lord in the path of His ordinances," the path of obedience, as far as is possible to you. And is there any other way? Can the drunkard wait for Him while he abides at his cup? Can the thief wait for Him while he continues in his diabolical trade? Can any man indulging in absolute open sin find the Lord? Must he not, as the Saviour says, cut off that right hand, and pluck out that right eye? He never can cleanse his guilt, but he CAN cut off his hand, and when he does that, then the Holy Spirit will come in and apply the Blood, and do the cleansing.

Therefore, you perceive, I take the Gospel to be aiming not merely at saving, but *restoring* us. If it were merely to save me without restoring me, what would it do for me? As a moral agent, if the Gospel fails to PUT ME RIGHT it will fail eternally to make me happy; and if you were to transplant me before the throne, and put me down in the inner circle of archangels with a sense of wrong in my heart, being morally out of harmony with the laws of God, and the moral laws of the universe, I should be as miserable as if I were in hell, and should want to get away. I must be MADE RIGHT, as well as treated as if I were right. I must be changed as well as justified. This is the Gospel put as clearly in our text as it could be, and also the Epistles written by the Apostle Paul, the great expounder of the doctrine of justification by faith. It was through the lips of the glorified Lord Himself, after He had risen, to the great Apostle of the Gentiles, after the Gospel dispensation was fully opened, that this most unmistakable commission was given, " Unto whom now I send thee to open their eyes." What to ? Their sins. As Peter opened the eyes of the murderers of our Lord, on the Day of Pentecost, "Whom ye have crucified and slain," driving in the convicting truth of God until, in their agony, they cried out, "WHAT MUST WE DO?" He tore off the bandages which Satan had wrapped around them, and drove them as with the schoolmaster's lash, until he drove them to the Cross of the crucified One. "Open their eyes" —that is the first thing. Oh! how my soul has often shrunk and wept under the sense of the awful responsibility this brings upon us Christians. The world is asleep. Yes, friends, your relations, your neighbours—they are asleep. They are preoccupied. They are full of the world, and the things of the world. They will not think—they will not see —they will not look into the Word of Life. Your responsibility comes here tenfold. Go AND WAKE THEM! You CAN DO IT, if you have the Holy Ghost in you!

Some people would have said to the Lord Jesus, " What a great deal you are making of human agency, for, after all, Paul is but a man, and you are setting him to open the eyes of the unconverted, and turn them from darkness to light, and from the power of Satan unto God. Are you not making too much of human effort? But the Lord Jesus knew what He was about. He knew that Paul had a power in him which every really renewed child of God has—the Holy Ghost—to equip him for this work; and He says,

"Unto whom now I send thee to *open their eyes.*"
Go and awake them to a sense of their danger. Take
them, metaphorically speaking, by the collar and shake
them and make them realise their peril, as you would
if they were asleep in a burning house!! And then
when you have awakened them, what are you to do?
Leave them alone? No, no, for Christ's sake, no!
Take hold of them by the mighty power of your moral
suasion and zeal, and love, and energy, and turn them
right round from sin and Satan unto God.

Jesus Christ set Paul to do this, and *Paul did it.*
He says, " Knowing, therefore, the terror of the Lord,
we persuade men." His was no meek and mild
putting of the truth, and leaving people to do as they
liked. " Knowing, therefore, the TERROR of the Lord,
we PERSUADE men, because we thus judge that if one
died for all, then were all dead ; " and, oh! what
success the Lord gave him in his desperate enterprise.
What multitudes did he persuade, and succeed in
turning round from darkness to light, and from the
power of Satan unto God! Turn them round! 'Oh!
but,' you say, 'if they are turned round from darkness,
which represents evil, to light, which represents
righteousness, are they not saved?' No, not yet.
This is only the change effected in their will, which is
beautifully exemplified by Paul in Romans vii.—
willing to keep the law, willing to obey God, willing
to do His will, and follow Him; yea, struggling, but
yet unable; though they are brought round from the
voluntary choice or embrace of evil, and the voluntary
service of the Devil, round to the voluntary choice
and embrace of righteousness and the service of God,
they are not yet *able* to do it

Now, friends, don't say I said they *were* able. Don't misrepresent me, as some people do. I will try to be clear, and I say *there is all the difference in the world between* BEING WILLING TO LET JESUS CHRIST SAVE ME FROM MY SINS, AND SAVING MYSELF FROM THEM. It is exactly this change in the attitude of the will which God demands as a CONDITION OF THE EXERCISE OF HIS POWER. It is so in all the miracles. "Wilt thou be made whole?" He says to the man with the withered hand, "Stretch out thy hand." The man might have said, 'Lord, what an unreasonable request. Are you come to mock me in my misery?' Oh! but Jesus Christ knew what He wanted in the man. He wanted the response of the MAN'S WILL. He wanted the man to say, 'Yes, Lord;' and when He said that, the Lord put the strength into the shoulder-bone, and He stretched it out, and it was made whole. There are many souls just there—they will not say, 'Yes, Lord,' to some condition which the Spirit puts upon them. I could give you some heart-rending illustrations on this point. I am satisfied that this Gospel-enlightened England of ours is full of people just at this point, who come crying, and praying, and longing, as they call it, after God. They come up to Jesus Christ again and again. They try to believe; they want to follow Him, but they are kept back by the right hand and the right eye which the Holy Ghost has told them they must cut off and pluck out before He will receive them. They will not do it, and so they are ever learning, and never able to come to a knowledge of the truth. You must renounce evil in your will. You must *will* to "obey the truth." You must say, 'Yes, Lord.'

I remember, on one occasion, in the West of England,
I had been delivering week-day morning addresses. We
had a blessed meeting on this particular day. We
began at half-past ten, and the Lord was so with us
that He supplied the want of refreshment till we had
it at 5.30. He made up for the want of dinner or tea.
A gentleman was there, with whose appearance I was
struck. He was tall, and intelligent, a man of about
forty or forty-five. He knelt down without any emotion,
more than deep solemnity, at the end of the Communion rail. I had been talking about the reason
people walked in darkness—controversy with the Holy
Spirit. I said to him, ' My dear sir, have you had a
' controversy with the Holy Spirit ? ' ' Yes,' he said
' I have had one for fifteen years. I am ashamed to
' say it, and it has eaten up all the joy and power of
' my Christian life, and I have been a useless cumberer
' of the ground.' I did not know till afterwards that he
was a deacon of the church, and had come up there in
the sight of all the congregation. I said, ' Well, my
dear sir, you know the Gospel as well as I do. It is of
no use to preach faith to you until you are willing to
renounce your idol.' He said, most emphatically, ' I
know it.' I said, ' Are you willing ? ' Oh, with what
tenacity the human heart holds on to its idols! Though
he had come up to the rail in the face of that
congregation, so deeply was he under the power of the
Spirit, yet he hesitated. I said, ' Well, my dear sir,
you must make up your mind. In your case, it is
between the choice of this, whatever it may be, and
Christ ; ' and I retired under the pulpit pillars for a
minute, and left him to himself and the Lord. I lifted
up my heart to God for him, and then I went back, and

said, ' Will you renounce it ? ' and, lifting up his eyes
to heaven, and, bringing his hand down upon the
Communion rail, he said, ' By the grace of God, I do,'
and his whole frame heaved with agony, but he stepped
into immediate liberty.   His blessed Saviour was
waiting with arms wide open.   There was only this
accursed thing which had stood between them, and
when he trampled it under his feet, and was willing to
forsake it, as a natural consequence, he sprang into the
everlasting arms, and received the assurance of salvation.
It was all over the town for the next fortnight.   People
remarked, ' Did you ever see such a change come over
a man, as has come over Mr. So-and-so ; he is like a new
man.   He prays in the prayer-meeting with such
fervour.   He was at the chapel doors, speaking to the
unconverted, and inviting them to come back.   He is
visiting up and down the town—why, he's a new man ! '
Was there any change in the Gospel ?   Had he received
any fresh light ?   It was only the old story—only that
he had put away the idol, and trampled under foot
that which was keeping the life-power of God out of
his soul.

Here is another case.   At some services in the West
of England, a gentleman, largely interested in an
unlawful business, came every night for five weeks, and
used to sit there, the picture of despair and wretched-
ness, till after ten o'clock.   He went on in this way
until his friends thought he would lose his reason.   He
was walking about his bedroom with his Bible open,
kneeling down every now and then, struggling and
wrestling and trying to believe ; but every time he
thought of this ungodly business which he could not
give up, despair seized him, for he thought of his

money—he thought of the consequences to his family; until at last he said, 'Money or no money, I will settle it.' He gave it up, came out, and got saved at once.

Now I think these illustrations make clear what I mean, by the abandonment, the turning from the embrace of evil to the embrace of righteousness as an indispensable condition of forgiveness. Hence the Holy Ghost has carefully matained this order—'to open their eyes and to turn them (round) from darkness to light, and from the power of Satan unto God that they may receive forgiveness of sins and an inheritance among them that are sanctified by faith that is in me." You see what a different thing this is to presenting Christ to people just as they are, where they are, *doing what they like.* You see what a different Gospel it comes to, insisting upon a thorough renouncement and abandonment of evil as a condition of Jesus Christ receiving the sinner. This was Paul's Gospel. Will you give me any other definition of it? Can you explain it in any other way? Paul goes on to show us, how *he* understood :—" Whereupon, Oh! King Agrippa, I was not disobedient unto the heavenly vision, but shewed first unto them of Damascus and at Jerusalem and then to the Gentiles, they should repent and turn to God, and do works meet for repentance." Was this like saying *" Only believe?"* without respect to any antecedent change of mind? Can anybody show me anything here in the slightest degree approximating to the Antinomian Gospel which has been grafted on to some other of Paul's utterances? And yet surely the Apostle could not contradict himself. His writings about faith must be in harmony with this most unmistakable putting of the Gospel to both Jews and Gentiles. Moreover, did he tell Agrippa and Festus to believe? No, he left them trembling at his words, because they were not willing to abandon their sins and put away the accursed thing; but to the Philippian gaoler, who said, "Men and brethren, what must I do?" and who brought them out and began to wash their stripes, thus doing works meet for repentance at once, he said, "Believe on the Lord Jesus Christ and thou shalt be saved." Ah; my friend, you may try to get hold of Christ to your dying hour and at the last be lost, while you are holding on to your idols. If he could have saved us after that fashion, we needed no Christ, we could have gone into heaven without a Saviour; but He came to save His people *from their sins,* and while you are in love with your sins, you may struggle and tremble as Agrippa and Felix did, and as the young Ruler did, and you will meet a similar fate. You must let go your idols and be willing that Jesus should come and save you; not down among the dirt and mud of sin, but lift you out of it: wash you: make you clean: and keep you clean: *circumcise your hearts;* and put His law in them; and then you shall know the gladness of His salvation!

I have some people writing to me in this condition. If they are here this afternoon, let me say to them— This is what you have to do—let go your idols and say as the gentleman said of whom I have told you, 'Poverty or no poverty, business or no business, position or no position, suffering or prosperity; never mind—Christ, Christ, I let go all for Thee!'

Have you forsaken evil? Have you cut off the right hand? Have you plucked out the right eye?

I have people coming to me in services of this character, groaning and sometimes worn to skeletons. They tell me they are in distress, they have got into bondage, they want the joy of the Lord and His daily fellowship; and when I ask the reason, they generally say 'Well, I dont know, but it seems to be want of faith.' Now, I say to such people:

'Now let us see what this want of faith arises from.' There must be a cause. I am afraid that sin lieth at the door, and when we come to close quarters, we generally find there is some idol, some course of conduct, or some *doubtful* conduct which keeps God out of the soul, and when this is confessed and renounced people get the presence of God and go away rejoicing in Him. It is so in nearly every case. God does not arbitrarily withdraw Himself from His people. He wants to dwell with them. We are His proper abode. He has promised to come and abide with his people, and if He does not, depend upon it there is something in the temple offensive to Him, something with which he will not dwell. Will you put that away, and consecrate your hearts this day unto the Lord to be His temple, His temple only, and leave consequences with Him? He will be able to look after His own.

Then, lastly, when you have come to this decision, then look and live; take the final leap into the arms of a crucified Saviour. With some souls who have been the subjects of the drawings of the Spirit for years, the difficulty is in the surrendering of their wills. They have learned to reason with God; they have lost the little children's way; they are afraid to take the final leap, and there they stand before the Cross, not conscious of anything between them and

Christ. What are *you* to do? What Paul told the Philippian gaoler to do—" Believe on the Lord Jesus Christ; " and you say, " What is that, and how am I to believe ? " Wonderful how it has got mystified! Believe what ? That He just means what He says; and that when you come, He does receive—not He will to-morrow, nor He did yesterday, but that He does now, this moment. When did He receive the sinners who came to Him on earth ? When they came. Just the same will He receive you. 'Oh, but,' you say, 'I do not feel right.' No, of course not. Do you not see, you are to be saved *by faith*. If you are to be saved by faith, you must exercise faith before you will be saved. If it is by faith you are to be saved, you must believe first, and be saved afterwards; if it is only the next second. ' But,' you say, ' I do not feel it.' No, but you will feel it when *you have got it*. You must believe it before you get it, on the testimony of His Word—" I will in no wise cast you out; " "Him that cometh ; " 'Now I come, Lord, I come. I have put away my idols ; I have put away everything that consciously stood between me and Thee. I *will* to serve Thee, I will to follow Thee, I will to put my *neck under Thy yoke for ever*, asking no more questions, but being willing for Thee to lead me whithersoever Thou wilt. Now, Lord, I come—Thou dost receive.' Leap off the poor old stranded wreck of your own effort, or your own righteousness, or your own sinfulness, or your own unworthiness, or anything else of your own, into the glorious lifeboat. It is on the top of the wave this afternoon—another step, and you will be in—one bound, and you will feel the loving arms of your

Saviour around you. Faith is trust, TRUST. He will
do for you what He promised. Believe that God does
*now accept you wholly for the sake of the sacrifice of
His blessed Son;* that He justifies you freely from all
things from which you could not be justified by the
law. You stand a condemned, guilty, hell-bound
criminal, and nothing but His free, sovereign mercy
can save you. Throw yourself upon this, and the
moment you do so in real faith you will be saved.
Perhaps you will say, as a curate of the Church of
England, writing to me last week said, 'I refuse to be
saved by logic.' Amen, amen. So did I, and I
struggled for six weeks because I refused to be saved
by logic — because I *would* have a living, personal
Christ. I admire your decision, my brother, if you
are here, but let this logic help you: nevertheless,
Jesus Christ has promised, if I come, that He will
receive me—then, I do come, and He does receive me,
for He cannot lie. Let that help you. Faith is not
logic, but logic may help faith.

Oh! how I should rejoice if some of you were to
launch into the arms of Jesus this afternoon. It often
happens that while I am speaking souls *do* get into
the ark of God's mercy, and come, or write to tell me
afterwards that the Spirit has come, and he is crying
" Abba Father," and now they KNOW they have passed
from death unto life. They don't want logic then.
It is a matter of demonstration with them. When
you have come up to the place where saving faith is
possible to you, you have no more to do, no more to
suffer, no more to pay. By simple trust we are saved.
This is the way every saint on earth was saved. This
is the way every saint in glory was saved. This is

the way we are kept saved too, by LIVING DAILY, OBEDIENT FAITH. The Lord help you just now. Let the idol go. Put away the ungodly companion. Give up the unlawful business, or the worldly conformity. Put away whatever has stood between you and Jesus. Trample it under foot and press through the crowd of difficulties as the woman did, and go right up and touch Him with this touch of faith, and you shall LIVE and KNOW THAT YOU ARE HEALED. Then this Gospel will be good news indeed to you, and Jesus will be the author of eternal salvation to you, because you OBEY HIM!

ADAPTATION OF MEASURES.

ADAPTATION OF MEASURES.

I HAVE chosen, this afternoon, five or six different passages all exhibiting the principle of Adaptation, on which I am to speak. The first is I. Cor. ix. 20-22 :—

> *" And unto the Jews I became as a Jew, that I might gain the Jews, to them that are under the law, as under the law, that I might gain them that are under the law ; to them that are without law, as without law (being not without law to God, but under the law to Christ), that I might gain them that are without law."*

To them that are without law as without law ; but here he carefully guards himself by a parenthesis, lest he should seem to favour a lawless Antinomian Gospel, "not without law to God," not independent of the great moral law, "but under the law to Christ," in which is fulfilled ALL LAW.

> *" To the weak became I as weak, that I might gain the weak · I am made all things to all* men, *that I might by all means save some "*

"To the weak became I as weak,"—masterpiece of human humility! Most people want to appear strong, but here is a man coming down, and appearing a weak man, that he might win the weak. *That* is the humility of Jesus Christ :—

The Lord give us the like spirit! Again, I. Cor. xii. 4-6 :—

> *" Now there are diversities of gifts, but the same spirit ; and there are differences of administration, but the same Lord; and there are diversities of operations, but it is the same God which worketh all in all "*

Some people want the Spirit to work in everyone
alike, and in all times the same, but He *chooses* to
have diversities.   Again, Galatians iii. 27, 28 :—

> " *For as many of you as have been baptised into Christ have*
> *put on Christ   There is neither Jew nor Greek : there is*
> *neither bond nor free : there is neither male nor female :*
> *for ye are all one in Christ Jesus* "

That is, so far as the privileges, duties, and
obligations of Christ's kingdom are concerned, there
is neither nationality nor sex ; and Galatians v. 6 :—

> " *For in Jesus Christ neither circumcision availeth anything, nor*
> *uncircumcision ; but faith which worketh by love.*"

All mere ordinances and ceremonies come under
the Apostle's term "circumcision."   And II. Timothy
iv. 2 :—

> " *Preach the word : be instant in season, out of season : reprove,*
> *rebuke, exhort with all longsuffering and doctrine.*"

What a hue-and-cry there is because we Salvation
Army people save men "out of season !"   And Jude
22, 23 :—

> " *And of some have compassion, making a difference : and others*
> *save with fear, pulling them out of the fire* "

'Oh, no,' say some of our conventional friends, 'you
should not make a difference.'   Nevertheless, in all
these six texts, the principle of *Adaptation* is most
distinctly laid down.

Now, we have spent the two last Sabbath afternoons
in trying to point out our view of the characteristics
of a pure Gospel, and I think we have succeeded in
doing this so clearly that no person who followed us
carefully, can imagine for a moment that we would
hold, or teach any adaptation of the Gospel itself.
As we stated before, we deemed this so above all
adaptation—so above any change, that we would not

be responsible for transposing its order, much less altering its matter, that we would not take a dot off one of the "i's," so sacredly intact do we believe the Gospel of Christ in its matter ought to be kept. We believe also that the ORDER of God ought to be strictly maintained; that it is as rational and true in philosophy as it is in divinity; and that the way the Spirit operates upon the minds of men is just the same as ever. This we clearly and most carefully pointed out, so that what we have to say this afternoon, you will please bear in mind, has nothing to do with the GOSPEL MESSAGE ITSELF. We have tried to show our idea (or what we believe to be the Holy Spirit's idea) of a pure Gospel; but when we come to speak of modes and measures, that is quite another thing. I think, from the texts we have read, and from many others equally plain and relevant, that we find a most easily-gathered truth running all the way through the New Testament, namely, that forms and ceremonies are nothing except as they embody and express real spiritual life and truth. That circumcision is nothing, and that uncircumcision is nothing; baptism is nothing, and being unbaptised is nothing; the Lord's Supper is nothing, and abstaining from the Lord's Supper is nothing, in itself, as a matter of form, for he embraces under circumcision all mere outward forms and ceremonies; all these are nothing, but "KEEPING THE COMMANDMENTS OF GOD:" that is, you may have all these performed upon you, and regularly perform them yourselves, and be but sounding brass and tinkling cymbals, if you keep not the commandments of God; for circumcision availeth nothing, in another place, and uncircumcision availeth

nothing, but faith—of what sort?—that WORKETH BY
LOVE: that proves its obedience by its deeds.   Therefore, we start with that fundamental truth lying
clearly before us in every page of the New Testament,
that forms and ceremonies, whatsoever they may be,
are nothing except as they embody and represent REAL
SPIRITUAL LIFE, and truth and action—*action!*   Now,
it was the great sin—the crowning condemnation of
the Jews—that they had frittered away the spirituality
and practical bearing of the Divine Law, clinging to
those forms and ceremonies which were instituted only
to embody and symbolise it.   Would to God they had
let go the form when they let go the spirit.   Jesus
Christ wishes they had.   He tells them it would have
been far better.   He told them they were children of
the Devil, notwithstanding their holding on to their
relationship to Abraham and all the outward forms
and ceremonies of their ritual.

They had better have come out and avowed themselves unbelievers, than have gone on professing to be
the children of God, while they were doing the work
of the Devil.   But they would not receive this
teaching.   It was too cutting for them, and so they
would not have it.   It was true, nevertheless.   They
held on to the form whilst the spirit had gone.   They
were "making clean the outside of the platter, but
within they are full of extortion and excess, appearing
beautiful outward, but within they are full of dead
men's bones and all uncleanness."   And, dear friends,
all corpses are very much alike, when the spirit is
gone out of them—one is found to be about as good
as another.

Alas! there is this tendency still in our fallen

human nature. It is so much easier, or Satan makes
it look so much easier, to an unregenerate man, to
rest in a form, than to seek till he finds the spiritual
grace which that form represents. That is to say, it
is so much easier for an unregenerate man to be
circumcised, or to be baptised, as the case may be, to
partake of the Lord's Supper, to keep outwardly the
Sabbath Day, to abstain from acts of immorality and
open sin, and to be decently moral and religious—all
this he can understand and do for himself, and it
looks to him so much easier, and so it is, in the first
instance, than bringing his evil, unregenerate heart to
God for Him to circumcise it, and write His law in it,
as He promises to do under the new covenant.

Now, that is what God wants every man to do. He
wants him to bring this *heart to Him,* and let *Him
renew it.* He says, " I will circumcise your hearts to
keep my law." But, no! the unregenerate man rests
in the outward form. He will not be at the trouble
to sacrifice his idols, and cry mightily unto God. He
will not seek until he attains the fulfilment of these
promises ; so he sits down and rests in the form.

Alas! alas! how many thousands in this so-called
Christian England of ours to-day are just there. They
have got the form ; they are like the Jews—they are
Pharisees with a Christian creed instead of a Jewish,
the same in CHARACTER, only different in name. That
is all the difference, hanging on to the creed of Jesus
Christ, while they know nothing of its spirit, the form
without the power; and they deny their professed
Lord every day. Oh! are there any of this class here?
My friend, my friend, if you never find it out until you
come to die, you will find it out then, but it may be too

late. May God, the Holy Spirit, help you to find it out this afternoon, and bring that unrenewed, unrepentant, evil heart of yours to the Cross; bring it to God, and wait, and weep, if need be, and struggle, and knock, and cry, as He tells you, until He does renew it and write His law in it; then the outward form will be the expression of the inward grace. Then the fruit will be good, because it springs from a good root inside. The Lord help you!

This tendency to rest in form is just as great as ever, and, instead of putting away their idols, and bringing their conscience to be cleansed and kept clean by the precious blood, prayerfully and carefully walking before God, striving in all things to please Him, people get an outside form, but LIVE just like the world around them, calling Jesus, "Lord, Lord," but doing not the things that He says. Now, I say that a pure Gospel requires that we bring our evil HEARTS to God to be renewed, and that we resolutely put away our idols, and that we wait on Him by the Cross until He renews our motives, tempers, tendencies, feelings, and dispositions, and makes us new creatures in Christ Jesus. Instead of doing this, people go on being circumcised or baptised, as the Jews did, and they call themselves "Israel," as they did; whereas, of the spiritual Israel they are utterly ignorant. They are the children of Hagar (as Paul says), and not the children of the promise. May the Lord help you to come and be made children of the promise!

Now, as in the individual, there is such a tendency to rest in form, so in the Church collectively; hence this tendency to a formal religion. Just as it was with the Jews—their Temple service and the paraphernalia

of Judaism—was all in all to them, and they thought
that Jesus Christ was the most awfully severe and
uncharitable person who ever appeared on the face of
the earth, because He told them the truth. And the
same class of character presents the same attitude
now. We shall see when we get to the Judgment-
seat of Christ which is the true charity—that which
covers up things, or that which tears off the bandages,
and shows people their hypocrisy and, as we have just
read, reveals to them the secrets of their hearts. I
fear that we are very largely in the same condition
as the Jews were when Christ came. I say " very
largely," for I know that there are grand and glorious
exceptions ; but I speak of the great whole, and I
am backed up in this opinion by some of the most
thoughtful and spiritual men of this age. It is the
lamentation everywhere—this formality and death.
It reaches us from all parts of the land, yea, from
all parts of all lands. I once heard a great divine,
a leader of spiritual thought in his day, who has
recently passed to heaven, say, " I consider that the
writings of the Prophets are far more applicable to
the state of the churches now than the writings of
the New Testament, for we are in the same lapsed
and fallen condition, as churches, as Israel of old was."
So many think, and so many teach.

If this be the case, WHAT IS TO BE DONE ?
What would strike you should be done in this state
of comparative—spiritual eclipse ? Evidently it would
be madness to *go on as we are.* That will mend
nothing ! Somebody must strike and do something
worthy of the emergency. " There is no improving
the future, without disturbing the present," and the

difficulty is to get people to be willing to be disturbed! We are so conservative by nature—especially some of us. We have such a rooted dislike to have anything rooted up, disturbed, or knocked down. It is as much the work of God, however, to "root out, and to pull down, and to destroy," as "to build and to plant;" and God's real ambassadors frequently have to do as much of the one kind of work, as of the other. This is not pleasant work ; but what is *necessary* to be done? Is it not manifestly necessary that we should go back to the simplicity, and SPIRITUALITY of the Gospel, and to the early modes of propagating it amongst men?

On the two last Sunday afternoons we tried to show what was the pure Acts of Apostles Gospel—calling men to forsake their sins, to cast away their idols, come out from the world of the ungodly and be separate in order that their sins might be forgiven, and that God might receive them, and they become His sons and His daughters. Last Sunday we spoke of faith and what it would do for us.

Now, with respect to the outward manifestations and propagation of the Gospel it is equally necessary to go back. We have such a heap of rubbish to carry away—the accumulated traditionalism of ages to go through and dig under—that it sometimes takes a considerable amount of time, and force of character, and a great deal of the Spirit of God to enable us to do it. Nevertheless, it must be done if we are to reach a better state of things.

It seems to me, in order to do this we should not shrink from a recognition of our lapsed and fallen condition. That was what the Jews did at the teaching of Jesus. They would not have His reproach. They would not have the light because it condemned them. They rejected it. They persisted they were the children of Abraham—the children of the promise. They persisted they were all right, and they pointed to the Temple and to their ceremonialism as a proof of it ; they would not have His testimony, would not admit that they were wrong. Do not let us imitate them. Let us recognise this state of things. Let us look it fairly in the face. Honesty is always the best policy both in spiritual and in temporal things. There is nothing gained by ignoring a disagreeable truth. It is best to face it. Now there it is and the best way is to hail any ray of light that comes to us from any part of the heavens, even though a carpenter should bring it, as He brought it to them—or a fisherman, or a woman. Never mind—let us hail the light and apply it to ourselves. Let us bring our hearts and lives out into its blaze, and examine them by it, and improve it to our own salvation and to the salvation of others. If the Jews had done that, they would have been saved, and their nation. "If thou hadst known, even thou, at least in this thy day,"—this twelfth hour of the last day—"the things that belong unto thy peace ; but now"—because of thy obstinate rejection—"they are hid from thine eyes." The Lord help us to take the light home to ourselves, each one.

We have seen that it is clearly laid down in the texts I have read this afternoon, that the law of adaptation is the only law laid down in the New Testament with respect to modes and measures. I challenge anybody to find me any other. While the Gospel message is laid down with unerring exactness,

we are left at perfect freedom to adapt our measures
and modes of bringing it to bear upon men to the
circumstances, times, and conditions in which we live
—free as air. " I became all things to all men." The
great Apostle of the Gentiles who had thrown off the
paraphernalia of Judaism years before, yet became as
a Jew that he might win the Jews. The great, strong,
intellect became as a weak man, that he might win the
weak.   He conformed himself to the conditions and
circumstances of his hearers, in all lawful things, that
he might win them ; he let no mere conventionalities,
or ideas of propriety, stand in his way, when it was
necessary to abandon them.   He who was brave as a
lion, and hailed a crown of martyrdom like a conquering
hero, as he was, yet was willing to submit to anything,
when the requirements of his mission rendered it
necessary.   He suffered his limbs to be ignominiously
thrust into a basket, and himself let down over the wall
when necessary, for the success of his work.   He
adapted himself to the circumstances.   He was instant
in season and out of season.   Oh ! what a hue-and-cry
there is about out-of-season Christianity ; " of some
making a difference "—pulling them out of the fire by
the hair of the head, if needful ! Never mind—*save
them*, SAVE THEM.   That is the great desideratum.
Save them—pulling them out of the fire.   Adapt your
measures to your circumstances and to the necessities
of the times in which you live.   Now, here it seems to
me that the Church—I speak universally—has made a
grand mistake, the same old mistake which we are so
prone to fall into, of exalting the traditions of the elders
into the same importance and authority as the Word of

God, as the clearly laid down principles of the New Testament.

People contend that we must have quiet, proper, decorous services. I say, WHERE IS YOUR AUTHORITY FOR THIS? Not here. I defy any man to show it. I have a great deal more authority in this book for such a lively, gushing, spontaneous, and what you call disorderly, service, as our Army services sometimes are, in this 14th of Corinthians than you can find for yours. The best insight we get into the internal working of a religious service in Apostolic times is in this chapter, and I ask you—is it anything like the ordinary services of to-day? Can the utmost stretch of ingenuity make it into anything like them? But even that is not complete. We cannot get the order of a single service from the New Testament, nor can we get the form of government a single church. Hence one denomination think theirs is the best form, and another theirs; so Christendom has been divided into so many camps ever since; but this very quarrelling shows the impossibility of getting from the New Testament the routine, the order, and the fashion of mere modes. They cannot get it, because it is not there!! Do you think God had no purpose in this omission? The form, modes, and measures are not laid down as in the Old Testament dispensation. There is nothing of this stereotyped routinism in the whole of the New Testament. Why? Now there may be some who may have difficulties in this matter. I said to a gentleman, who came to me with this and that difficulty about our modes and measures, 'I will meet your difficulties by bringing them face to face with

the bare principles of the New Testament. If I
cannot substantiate and defend them by that I will
give them up for ever. I am not wedded to any
forms and measures. To many of them I have been
driven by the necessities of the case. God has driven
me to them as at the point of the bayonet, as well as
led me by the pillar of cloud, and when I have
brought my reluctance and all my own conventional
notions, in which I was brought up like other people,
face to face with the naked bare principles of the
New Testament, I have not found anything to stand
upon! I find things here far more extravagant and
extreme, than anything we do—looked at carefully.'
Here is the principle laid down that you are to adapt
your measures to the necessity of the people to whom
you minister; you are to take the Gospel to them in
such modes and habitudes of thought and expression
and circumstances, as will gain for it from them a
HEARING. You are to speak in other tongues—go
and preach it to them in such a way as they will
look at it and listen to it! Oh! in that lesson we
read what beautiful freedom from all set form and
formula there was! What freedom for the gushing
freshness, enthusiasm, and love of those new converts!
What scope for the different manifestations of the
same spirit. Everything was not cut and dried.
Everything was not pre-arranged. It was left to the
operation of the Spirit, and the argument that this
has been abused, is no argument against it, for then
you might argue against every privilege. Here is
abundant evidence that these new converts, each one,
had opportunity to witness for Jesus, opportunity
and scope to give forth the gushing utterance of his

soul, and tell other people, how he got saved, or the
experience the Holy Ghost has wrought in him. And
look at the result! " If there come in one that
believeth not, or one unlearned, he is convinced of all,
he is judged of all; and thus are the secrets of his
heart made manifest, and so *falling down on his face,*
he will worship God, and report that God is in you of
a truth." What unkind things have been said of The
Salvation Army, because people have fallen on their
faces under the convicting power of the Spirit at our
meetings, but you see this is Apostolic! And, oh,
friends, what a glorious service this would be! You
say, it would look so strange. More the pity. More
the pity that this natural, easy, domestic, familiar kind
of testimony and witnessing of divine things should
have become strange. May it not be because the
experience which prompted it has become strange?
May it not be that there is no more desire to testify
because there is little to testify about? May it not
be that there is want of the utterance of the Holy
Spirit through the tongue because there is less of it
in the soul? Oh! then, should we not make haste
back to those days of simplicity and power? Should
we not pray to be set free from the traditionalism and
routinism in which Satan has succeeded in lulling
us to sleep? I ask any saved man—Do you not
remember the gushing love and enthusiasm of your
first-found liberty? how you longed to tell everybody,
and if you had been placed in such circumstances as
these Corinthian converts, how gladly you would have
testified to what Jesus had done for you. It was only
the repressing, keeping down, and ultimately, I am
afraid the all-but extinguishing of the Holy Spirit's

urgings that has led to the state in which many of you now are, and also to the dead way in which many of our services are conducted.

Now, let us look fairly at these things. I maintain that the only qualification—the only indispensable qualification—for witnessing for Christ is the Holy Ghost. Paul, expressly, over and over again, abjures all merely human equipment. He expressly declares that these things were not the power, even where they existed, but that it was the Holy Ghost. Therefore, give me man, woman, or child, with the Holy Ghost, full of love and zeal for God, and I say it is a great strength and joy to that convert to testify to the Church and to the world, and it is the bounden duty of the Church to give him the opportunity to do so. The Lord is going to demonstrate in this land, that He is not going to evangelise it by finished sermons and disquisitions, but by the simple *testimony of people saved from sin and the Devil, by His power and His grace.* He is going to do it by WITNESSING, as He began.

Now, I say, read your New Testament on this point, and you will be struck with the amazing amount of evidence for this unconventional kind of service. The world wants some more PENTECOSTS. When shall Peters and Marys be so filled with the Spirit that they cannot help telling what God has done for them— male and female, men, women, and children—like the woman of Samaria, who, when she had found Him of whom Moses and the Prophets wrote, went and fetched her fellow-townsmen and women to hear him. He wishes you to do the same, and this is the way the Lord is going to gather out His great and glorious kingdom in these latter days by the power of testimony in the Holy Ghost. He only wants witnesses to be able to go and say, " We speak that we do know "— *that* is the qualification. The Lord is multiplying such witnesses. Bless His holy name.

But you may say—what did the Master Himself do? Well, he adopted these very measures. I was so struck with this, when someone said, " Why, you are sending people to preach who cannot read or write." For a moment I was staggered, but I asked him, " How many of the Apostles do you suppose could read and write when they were first sent out ? " And then it was the questioner's turn to be staggered. There is no reason to suppose, with but two or three exceptions, that any of them could. Education then was far more uncommon than now. It was not reading and writing that was the great qualification for preaching Christ; it was KNOWING AND SEEING ! It was not the power of eloquence, but it was being able to cast out devils, that was the test. Give me somebody able to cast out devils, and I don't care whether they can read or write, or put a grammatical sentence together. That is of no consequence whatever. Why did not Jesus Christ call the doctors and scribes of His day? There were plenty of them—highly educated men with trained and disciplined minds. He was amongst them in the Temple, when He was twelve years old. He knew them. How was it He did not select these ? He who could have commanded a legion of angels, could surely have commanded a few scribes and doctors to go to preach the Gospel. Why not ? He acted on the law of adaptation. He wanted His Gospel preached to the great

5

masses—not to the select few. Not to the educated
"upper ten," but to the great masses of mankind
How was He to have His Gospel so preached, but by
men like unto themselves? They fled from the
educated doctors. They would not listen to the
doctors, and they will not now. It may be very
wicked, and obstinate, and foolish, but such is the fact
—they never have and they never will. Hence, Jesus
Christ, instead of working a miracle, which he never
did when it was unnecessary, chose the weak things
of the earth to confound the mighty. He would, in
the other case, have had first to have untaught all
those scribes and doctors almost all they had learned.
He would have had to set them free from the bonds of
traditionalism. He would have had to remould their
minds, and then equip them. There was no necessity
for this, when He found the fishermen ready to His
hand. They were just the men He wanted. They
only required tempering with the Holy Ghost, and
they were ready for the work. They thought as the
people thought; they spoke with and associated with
the people, and, in fact, were of them. As He wanted
the masses of men evangelised, He chose men from
amongst the masses to evangelise them. Here was
infinite wisdom. "I thank Thee, oh, Father, that
Thou hast hid these things from the wise and prudent,
and hast revealed them unto babes. Even so, Father,
for so it seemed good in Thy sight." But He had a
purpose in it, and the purpose was this—that the
Gospel might be propagated in all climes and
conditions of men, through any kind of an agent—
Greek, Jew, Barbarian, Scythian, man, woman, child.
Any person who has experienced its power in their

souls may go and speak it to anybody they can get to
hear them and everywhere! We are free as air and
sunlight as to our choice of agencies, and it is time
the Church woke up to this. The Lord have mercy
on us! Is there not work enough to do? It makes
my ears tingle and burn with shame when I hear
people saying, ' You must not send agencies here and
there, and we can't have our organisation interfered
with.' I say, ' Are all the sinners converted in your
neighbourhood?' Nay; has every poor, lost, wretched
soul heard the name of Jesus, and the testimony of
His Gospel? Are there not teeming thousands round
about you who never heard His name, and who care
nothing for Him, who live every day trampling His law
under their feet? *For Christ's sake, send somebody
after them.* If they will not have your doctors of
divinity and your polished divines, get hold of
fishermen and costermongers and send them! Let
the people have a chance for their souls. Let them
hear, for if they hear not, how shall they believe. Oh,
they are dying for lack of knowledge—they are,
friends; thousands, are dying for the lack of knowledge. It is quite a common thing for us to get
people into our services who say, ' I never knew there
was anything so pretty as that in the Bible. I didn't
know you were reading from the Bible. We never
heard anything like that before.' Hundreds of men in
this country were never in a place of worship, save to
be christened or to be married, and a good many, sad to
say, are living without being married. While we
have been standing UPON OUR DIGNITY, WHOLE GENERA-
TIONS HAVE GONE TO HELL!—if the Bible is true. How
much longer shall we stand there? If Jesus had

stood upon His dignity He would never have come to die between two thieves. The whole work of redemption is a work of humiliation, self-sacrifice, and suffering; and if we are not willing to follow Him in that, we may as well give up professing His name.

The Lord help us to go down, down amongst the fishermen, amongst the poor, the weak, the unlearned, the vulgar, to " condescend to men of low estate."

ASSURANCE OF SALVATION

ASSURANCE OF SALVATION.

ROMANS viii. 3, 4.—"*For what the Law could not do, in that it was weak through the flesh, God sending His own Son in the likeness of sinful flesh, and for sin, condemned sin in the flesh That the righteousness of the Law might be fulfilled in us, who walk not after the flesh, but after the Spirit*"

I WILL try, by God's grace, as much as in me lies, to deal with this subject in a way that shall not provoke controversy. I do deplore this. I wish there was a way of improving the future without disturbing the present, but it is a misfortune, I suppose, that there is not, and, however carefully one may guard oneself in trying to lead the Lord's people higher, there is always somebody who will quibble and make objections and take exceptions. But we cannot help this. We must be true to our convictions of God's truth, and to what He has taught us, and revealed to us by His Spirit, for we speak the things that we do know, and do see, and do handle of the Word of Life. However, I will try to keep to ground on which I think all really spiritual people will be agreed. We may go a bit farther some day, but this afternoon we will just go so far as we believe every real disciple of the Lord Jesus will be willing to go with us, and, oh ! may the Holy Spirit give us one mind and help us to see in His light, and if there is anything we do not see in His light, oh ! that this very hour He may show it to us, for He knows that we are all willing to see, and only longing and desiring to know the whole truth, as it is in Jesus. Let every sincere soul put up this prayer for himself and for me, as I put it up for myself and for you, that the Holy Spirit may lead us into all truth, at any rate as far as it is important to our own salvation and our practical exhibition of the salvation of Christ to other people, for a dying world is hanging upon our skirts. They are looking at us to find out what religion is. They will not come to this Book. They will not even hear about it, but they are looking to us to find it out; how momentously important it is, therefore, that we should be truly living Epistles, known and read of all men. We *are* epistles, whatever sort of doctrine our lives teach. We cannot help ourselves, for while we profess to be the Lord's, we are living epistles, known and read of all men.

Specially, then, I want first to look at the 3rd verse of the 8th chapter. Now, I thought it would, perhaps, be the most profitable way to look at this subject, and would meet the experience of some who I know are here, to try to answer the question—

Wherein does the Law fail to save us? Then we shall be able to see *wherein and how Jesus Christ transcends the Law.*

First, then, the Law does not fail in giving a knowledge of sin, for it is by the Law, as the Apostle says, that I know sin. Without the Law I was dead, so dead in sin that I did not realise it at all. Its power was so complete over me that I did not realise it was sin, and, therefore, was asleep and comparatively happy; but when the commandment came, "sin revived and I died"—that is, to all hope of making myself righteous. The commandment showed me the awful chasm there was between me and it. The Holy

Commandment, just and pure and good—and myself unholy, impure, and unrighteous. A light from Sinai flashed upon it, and I died in despair and utter helplessness. Thus, I say, the Law does not fail in giving knowledge of sin, for it is by the Law that I *get* the knowledge of sin.

Secondly.—Neither does the Law fail in begetting a sense of guilt and condemnation on account of sin, for it is by the Law again that I get this. I not only get the knowledge of sin by the Law, but I get the sense of guilt and condemnation for sin by the Law, for the Law comes in and condemns me. It is the spirit of death and condemnation to me : it says, " you should have done this ; and because you have not done it, you shall die." I feel that the Law is just and good, and yet I feel that I do not keep it ; and, therefore, I have the sentence of condemnation upon me because I do not keep it. Then the Law does not fail in begetting a sense of condemnation and guilt on account of sin.

Thirdly.—Neither does the Law fail in producing *desire after righteousness and effort to attain it.* The Law begets in me the desire after righteousness, by contrasting my condition with the purity and holiness of God's law. I see the Law to be good and holy, I see it to be desirable, and I desire to attain the righteousness of the Law. I am speaking now of a convicted sinner, as the Apostle did when speaking of the same character. A convicted sinner sees the righteousness and beauty of the Law of God. He sees that it is holy, just, and good. He sees that it is intended to make him holy, just, and good, for the Law is not sin, as the Apostle says, but is ordained unto righteousness, which the sinner has failed to attain because of weakness, but struggles to attain. The first thing is to set himself to strive to attain the righteousness of the Law by his own efforts. This was the case with the Apostle. He longed to do what he could not, and he constantly did what he would not; and, as it was with the Apostle, so it is with every convicted sinner on earth. We were constantly longing after righteousness. We could not help looking on the beautiful, pure, and holy law of God, and we longed to keep it, and tried again and again, until we were tripped down again and again, and died in utter despair, never being able to attain it for ourselves and of ourselves. So you see the Law begets first a knowledge of sin ; secondly, it begets guilt and condemnation on account of sin ; and, thirdly, desire after righteousness and effort to attain it.

Thus far I think we must all be agreed. Wherein does the Law fail ? It does all this for me. It brings me right up, as it were, my schoolmaster lashing me right up to the cross, opening my eyes, creating intense desire after holiness and efforts for it, and then it just fails me. Where ? *At the vital point.* It cannot give me *power.* That is where the Law fails It cannot give me power to fulfil itself. I am strengthless through the weakness of the flesh and the sinfulness of my nature to keep it, and so I struggle and wrestle for power to keep it, but I have not power. " What the Law could not do, in that it was weak, God sent his Son to do," and I maintain HE DOES IT, and *that* is the one vital point where *the Son transcends the Law.*

Oh ! but there is a Gospel nowadays, a Law-Gospel. A great deal of the Gospel of these days never gets any

farther than the Law, and some people tell me that it
is never intended to do so, and then I ask, Wherein
does Christ Jesus advantage me ? What am I better
for such a Gospel, if my Gospel cannot deliver me from
the power of sin ? If through the Gospel I cannot get
deliverance from this "I-would-if-I-could religion,"
this "Oh!-wretched-man-that-I-am religion," wherein
am I benefited by it ? Wherein does your Gospel
do more for me than the Law ? The Law convinced
me of sin, and set me desiring and longing after
righteousness; but wherein is the superiority of Jesus
Christ, if He cannot lead me farther than that?
And I say, "Very well; your faith is vain, and Christ
died in vain, and you are yet in your sins, if that is all
it can do." If that is all Jesus Christ can do, His coming
is vain, and I am yet in my sins, and am doomed to
hug this dead corpse to the last, and go down to hell;
for death will never do for me, what the blood and
sacrifice of Jesus Christ cannot do for me. If Christ
cannot supersede the Law, then I am lost, and lost for
ever. Wherein then does this "Oh!-wretched-man
Gospel" supersede the Law ? Will anybody point it out
to me ?

Oh! but the *real* Gospel does. The Gospel that
represents Jesus Christ, not as a system of truth to be
received into the mind, as I should receive a system
of philosophy, or astronomy, but it represents Him as
a REAL, LIVING, MIGHTY Saviour, ABLE TO SAVE ME *now*.

I said to a lady once, who was seeking this deliverance, and who was struggling and wrestling, as I
kneeled by her side,—'Wait a minute. Suppose
Jesus Christ were here in His flesh, as He once was.
Suppose He were to come to your side now, and put

His hand upon you and say, 'Hush! I know your
desire; I see your heart; I know what you are
longing after. You are longing to be delivered from
everything that grieves Me, upon which My pure eyes
cannot look with allowance. You are wanting to be
brought into full conformity to My will, and that is
what I have come to do now. I have come to live
with you. I am taking up my abode under this roof,
and I will never leave your side. I will be with you
by day, and I will be with you by night. I will sit at
the dinner-table and tea-table with you, and walk out
with you, and go to bed with you, and rise up with
you. Don't be troubled. I will never leave you and
never forsake you.' Do you think if He were to come
and say that, you would be able to trust Him?'

'Oh! yes.'

' You would not be afraid?'

'Oh! no.'

'Now, what would it be that would save you?
Would it be the bodily presence of Jesus, which they
laid in the sepulchre, and which was as dead and
helpless as any other clay when the spirit was gone out
of it? NO It would be His spiritual presence,
would it not? and His spiritual eyes seeing you, and
His spiritual tongue speaking to you?'

' Yes.'

'Well, then, this is just the presence that He has
promised to be with everyone of His people, and now
He is here and able to do this, and will abide with you
and enable you to abide in Him, if you will just trust
Him; now, just trust Him.' And the Lord, by His
blessed Spirit, did take and reveal this truth unto her,

and just then and there she did leap into the arms of her Saviour and realise that He did save her.

Oh! friends, some people do not think we make enough of Christ. We make *all* of Christ, only it is a living Christ instead of a dead one. It is Christ in us, as well as for us. We believe in Christ for us, and we should not have been here at all, but for Christ for us up there for ever and ever, and nobody will hasten to throw the crown at His feet readier than I shall; but we believe in order to do it we must have Him in us, and if He is not in us, then it is sounding brass and tinkling cymbal to call upon Him for us. He must be in us. Christ in us as well as for us, and those whom He is not *in* He will not be *for*. If He dwell not " in you," ye are " reprobates." But Christ in us,—an ever-loving, ever-present, Almighty Saviour—is just able to do what the angels said He should do, that for which He was called Jesus, viz. :—to save His people from their sin.

Then how does He this ? Wherein does He supersede the Law ? Wherein does Christ do for me and wherein is He made to me, what the Law could not do or be to me ? We have seen what the Law could do and how far it could go. We have seen that it fails just at the vital point of power. Now, *how* does Christ become this power to me ? How is He made unto me—not for me, up in Heaven ; He is there too ; but how is He made unto me down here— wisdom, righteousness, sanctification, and redemption? How does He deliver His people from their sins ? How does He save us from the power of sin ? Now, you who are longing to get free, try and listen to me, and oh! may the HOLY GHOST TEACH US.

He does this, first, by giving

Assurance of Salvation. He saves and then He makes us conscious of the fact, which the Law could not do. All it could do was to set us struggling after it. It could not give us assurance. Now, by assurance, I mean the personal realisation of my acceptance in Christ; my acceptance by the Father; my present acceptance—I mean the inward assurance, which men and women find for themselves, or have revealed in themselves, which they know as a matter of consciousness. Not that which their minister tells them; not that which they learn from books; not even that which the Bible only tells them, for there are thousands of people who read the Bible, who are not saved, and who know they are not. You all know there are thousands of people, who believe it in vain.

I was walking down the Anxious Room at one of Mr. Moody's meetings, when two ladies came and said—

' Will you please speak to us ? '

I don't know why they came to me, except it was my plain dress which made them think, I ought to know, even if I did not, how to deal with souls. We took three chairs and sat down. The youngest was a lady about 30 or 33, and very intelligent, evidently an educated person, and the elder was an old lady, gorgeously attired. They sat down; and as to the younger one there was no mistake about her earnestness. Mr. Moody had been preaching on " The Cities of Refuge," and showing how the soul who desired to be saved had nothing to do and nothing to suffer, but only to run into the Cities of Refuge and be saved— a beautiful sermon for *convicted* sinners—and this lady said to me, almost passionately,—' How is it? there must be something wrong somewhere; there must be a mistake somewhere. I believe all that Mr. Moody has been saying, every word of it. I have believed every word since I was a little girl; in fact, I believe the whole of the New Testament—all about Jesus Christ, and I believe, moreover, that He died for me, and that He makes intercession for me, and yet I'm not saved a bit. I have no more power over sin than other people, and I know I am not saved. Now, what can be the reason? I am afraid it is want of faith.'

That is the universal resort to fall back upon by all souls in that condition I said—' Will you be honest with me. It is of no use coming to a spiritual doctor any more than to a physical doctor if you are not frank; you would only mislead him. If you really want to be saved, be honest with me, and I will try, by the help of the Spirit, to help you.'

' I do indeed want to be saved,' she said. ' I often go into my room, and weep, and struggle, and pray for hours. I try to believe. I think I have believed, and I come out and I am no better.'

' Oh,' I said to myself, ' alas! here is the experience of thousands.' ' Tell me, in these times when you say you go into your room, and struggle, and pray, and strive, and believe; tell me, is there anything that comes up before the eye of your soul as an obstacle and difficulty that has to be put away or embraced; anything that comes up and that the Spirit of God says ' you must sacrifice this, or cut off that, or do the other?' Just tell me that.'

She was quiet for a moment and speechless. She

waited; then she drew her breath and said—'Well, yes, I am afraid there is.'

'Ah!' I said, 'that is it; it is not want of faith, it is want of obedience. Now you may go on another ten years, going into your room, struggling and striving, and until you trample that under your feet, and say, 'Lord, I will follow Thee at all costs,' you will not be able to believe. I don't want you to tell me what it is; sufficient that you know it, and that the Lord knows it; but, after an experience of dealing with hundreds of souls just at this point, I tell you: you must give up that idol or embrace that cross, whatever it may be; I believe that here is the cause of your trouble.'

'Then,' she said, 'I will make no secret of it. I am the only member of an unconverted family that has any desire after God. My husband is a worldly, unconverted man, and I am in a worldly, unconverted, circle, and always when I come to the Lord Jesus, it comes up before me that I will have to confess Him and to live like a Christian, and I am not willing to do so.'

'Then, my dear lady, it is the old story over again of the Young Ruler. Now, you know, I should be untrue to your soul, if I were to go on plastering you with untempered mortar. There you are; make your choice. You cannot be a Christian, and not confess Christ. You cannot be a Christian, and not live like one before your unconverted relatives; and, therefore, if you are not willing to take up the cross and follow Him, you cannot become His disciple.'

Then I went down on my knees with her, and we talked and prayed, and, at last, she said,

'By the grace of God, I WILL confess Him.'

Bless the Lord! and the light of salvation soon gladdened her eye, for it shone through her face She found herself able to believe at once, and this is just the condition of thousands of souls. She got assurance then. She got saved. Before, she had being trying to believe she was saved, when she was not—quite a different thing to getting saved and then knowing it. People are told to believe this, that, and the other. As a gentleman said, at whose house I once stayed—

'I had a curious episode the other morning. I have had a gentleman here of some note in the evangelistic world for two or three days, and he came in the other morning at breakfast time and said, 'I am happy to tell you that both your gardeners are converted.' I was very thankful to hear it; and surprised to hear that the work had been so quickly and thoroughly done. Well, I was walking in the grounds, and saw one of the gardeners. 'John,' I said, 'I am glad to hear the happy news.' He didn't seem to know what I meant.

''What news, sir?'

''Well,' I hear you have given your heart to God this morning. You are converted, saved?'

''Well,' John said, 'I could hardly say that, sir.'

''Then what has happened? Something has happened in your experience — some change taken place?'

''Well,' he said, 'I don't hardly know that. The gentleman brought a Bible to me and read two or three verses, and asked me if I believed, and talked very nicely to me, and asked me again if I believed;

then I said I did, and then he said I was all right; but I can't say I feel any different.''

Now, I am afraid there has been sadly too much of that. There is all the difference between believing the letter of the Word and knowing that you are saved. I say, that man was *not* saved—was he? I say, the lady who spoke to me in the Anxious Room, was *not* saved—was she? And I say there are, alas! thousands to-day in just that position. They are not saved. They manifest it by their fruits. They confess it. They write it to me in their letters on the right hand and on the left. Members of churches ten, fifteen, and twenty years, some of them Ministers of the Gospel, and yet they tell me they are NOT SAVED!!

Thus, you see it is something more than the belief after all. It is something more than what my minister tells me, something more than what books tell me, and what the Bible tells me. It implies and includes this, but something more than this. It is believing in a living, personal, and almighty Saviour, and believing in Him now, and *that* faith brings the realisation. *The other brings nothing.* When people believe thus, the Spirit comes into their hearts, crying, "Abba, Father!" To them there is no condemnation. They have the witness of the Spirit that they are in Christ Jesus. The Spirit of the Son comes into their hearts, crying, "Abba, Father!" and they know by demonstration, by inward consciousness, that they have passed from death unto life. You see there is all the difference between the means of salvation and salvation itself. The means of salvation is not salvation. The means only brings salvation. "Thy faith hath saved thee." "By faith are ye saved," and when you are saved by faith then conciousness attests the fact. Your own spirit attests the fact, and God's Spirit attests the fact, and you know it beyond controversy. You have assurance, and this is the first indispensable condition of power over sin, for while I remain unassured of my salvation, oh! what power the Devil has over me. 'Oh,' he says, 'you're not saved at all. What is the good of your standing out on this point, for you are not saved at all. You may as well go all the way. You are under the power of sin, and may as well remain there. You have not got the witness of your salvation, and, therefore, what is the use of standing out here or there?' But when we have the witness of the Spirit in our souls of our acceptance with God, that He does now for Christ's sake pardon and receive us, what power it brings! This is what the old Divines called assurance of faith, a conviction wrought in the soul by the Holy Ghost that Jesus Christ has given Himself for me, that God has accepted that offering in view of my sin and transgression, and for its sake, and its sake *only*, has justified me freely from all things by which I could not be justified by the Law of Moses, and that in Him God becomes my Father, and now accepts me and looks upon me well pleased—a conviction wrought in my soul by the Holy Spirit; for, as the Apostle says, "No man can call Jesus 'Lord' but by the Holy Ghost." There must be the spiritual realisation of Him as Lord. Why, anybody can call Him "Lord." Tens of thousands of people call Him "Lord" nowadays, whom nobody supposes to have the Spirit. What

did he mean? He must have meant a confession of
Jesus out of a heart which has a revelation and
recognises its Lord; such a confession as Thomas
made when the conviction of His Master's Deity shone
into his doubting soul: " *My* Lord and *my* God."
To this relationship only the Holy Ghost can testify.
Don't ever tell anybody he is saved. I never do. I
leave that for the Holy Ghost to do. I tell them how
to get saved. I try to help them to the way of faith.
I will bring them up as close as ever I can to the
blessed broken body of their Lord, and I will try to show
them how willing He is to receive them, and I know
that when really they do receive Him, the Spirit of
God will tell them quickly enough that they are saved.
He will not want my assistance to tell that. I have
proved it in hundreds of cases. Nobody knows the
soul, but God. Nobody can see the secret windings of
the depraved heart, but God. Nobody can tell when
a full surrender is made, but God. Nobody can tell
when the right hand is cut off, or the right eye plucked
out, but God. Nobody can tell when a soul is whole-
hearted, but God, and as soon as He sees it, He will
tell that soul that it is saved; but, if God has not told
you, be up and stirring, and strive to make your calling
and election sure, for you are not saved yet, or you
would know it. What are you to believe unto? Hope?
Oh, dear no! you don't believe unto hope. Effort?
Oh, no! you had that before in the Law. SALVATION?
Yes! and if you " believe unto *salvation*" you will get
" *saved*," and if you are not saved, you have never
believed unto salvation. Instead of trying to make
yourself happy in this state of uncertainty and misery,
for Christ's sake, get up and get saved. It is a great

deal easier to get saved, than it is to make yourself believe you are saved, when you are not. The one is a philosophical impossibility; the other is a glorious possibility at any moment, when you get low enough before God, and give up all, and take His Son as your precious and almighty Saviour. God's Gospel is beautifully adjusted to the laws of our mental constitution. He who wrote, framed, and conceived it, created us, and He has made it like a key to fit the lock, and knows just the conditions that are necessary, and He has conformed His Gospel to those conditions.

My Friend, if you want to know you are saved, this is the only response I can give, and the only way I know, and I have talked to hundreds of souls of all grades and conditions, to many Ministers of the Gospel, deacons and leaders, in just this state. For years my labours were exclusively carried on in churches and chapels, where, naturally, church members have come, and they have told me by hundreds with their own lips that they have been members so many years and were never saved. I am not, therefore, speaking without experience in this matter. I tell you, when you " believe " in a Scriptural sense, you will get " saved " in a Scriptural sense. When you put out of your head all these new-fangled notions about faith, and cease to credit any faith that does not save the soul and bring it into conscious union with Jesus Christ, and resolve to have such a faith as will do that for you, then you will get salvation. I never in my life knew a soul come to that resolve who did not get saved. I have had people before me, who were worn almost to skeletons and were driven almost mad, and the first thing they have said has been, when I have asked the

reason, ' Oh! I have no faith. It is want of faith!'
This is the universal lament, and, when we have come
to close quarters, I have invariably found it has been
no such thing, but want of OBEDIENCE, which
spiritual teachers have not had the wisdom to discern,
as Christ did in the heart of the young Ruler, " one
thing thou lackest." He saw that young man's besetting sin to be covetousness. I do not know that He
would have said the same to every rich man, but in
the case of the young Ruler He saw that the love of
his possessions was so paramount, that unless he let
them go and made a clean sweep, he could not follow
Him and be a consistent disciple; and so He said,
" Sell all, and come, follow Me," and the young man
went away sorrowful; and, mark you, Jesus Christ did
not call him back, and yet he looked after him and
loved him. His great, benevolent, heart panted after
him, and He desired to have him; but He saw it would
be a greater evil to call him back and compromise the
conditions of salvation, than to let him be lost. And
yet, methinks, if there was any case in which a
compromise could be made, it would have been in this.
He did not do, as many would have done in our day—
call him back and say, ' Here, young man, I think I
have been a little too hard on you. You shall sell half,
and keep the other half and come and follow me.' Oh,
no! Everybody would be saved at that rate. There
would be no test of whole-hearted consecration to Him
then. If you can let people into heaven on terms like
these, they would be only too ready to close with them.
But whether ministers teach people the truth or not,
the Holy Ghost does; and He puts His finger on the
sore spot, and says, 'If you want to follow me, you will

have to renounce this, and give up that, or embrace
the other,' and if the soul says, 'No, Lord. I would
follow, but suffer me first to go and hug this idol'; then
Jesus Christ says, 'Very well, go!'' That is the sort
of faith most people are resting in.

I see we shall not get any farther in this address
than assurance of salvation. You are panting after it.
You are longing for it. You may have it. God wants
every one of His people to have it. Get saved, and you
will know it. Use your Heavenly Father's letter to
find your way up to Him. It is not the letter you are
to rest in : it is the God who wrote it. Use the letter
to get at the Spirit, for the letter will not save you—it
is the Spirit that saves you. Hug this volume to your
heart as the expression of your Father's will and the
record through which you are to believe on His Son,
but it is the Son who is to save you. People talk
about exalting Christ. I think this is His glory, that
He can save His people and make them know it, and
make them feel it, and carry them as He did Paul and
Silas through the prison and the stocks singing His
praises and make them unspeakably happy in His love.
Assurance of Salvation! All want it when they come
to die Why don't people get it while they live. Did
you ever know a professing Christian come to die, who
did not want it ? Did you ever know one dare to die
without it ? or, if you ever knew such, you know what
a miserable death it was. Then, I contend, that what
is necessary to die with, is necessary to live with.
Why not get it while you live? Assurance! Assurance!
And you can have it just now. Hallelujah! Amen.

HOW CHRIST TRANSCENDS
THE LAW.

HOW CHRIST TRANSCENDS THE LAW.

Romans vii. 4 —" *Wherefore, my brethren, ye also are become dead to the law by the body of Christ, that ye should be married to another, even to him who is raised from the dead, that we should bring forth fruit unto God*"

In answer to letters received since last Sabbath, I would just say that the writers tell me that they have been struggling for years for assurance; that they do receive the testimony of God concerning His Son; that they do believe that Jesus Christ died for their sins; still they have no peace or joy. I want you to mark well that assurance of salvation is the testimony of God's Spirit to a fact which has transpired, and if that fact has not transpired, God's Spirit will never testify to it. You may think you believe; but, oh, I feel sure numbers of people are deluded here. They think they believe because they receive into their minds the written record that God has given of His Son; but they have not believed and rested on the promise in such a way as to bring the witness of the *Spirit* They have stopped short of that. They have been satisfied with the *letter*.

Now, do not think, friends, that I underestimate the *letter*. Perhaps few of you, if any, value this word more than I do, but I have known very few of those who have rested merely in the letter (and I have known many do so), who, when I have come into close conversation with them, have not been miserably dissatisfied, unassured, sin-conquered souls; and that fact alone convinces me that there is something wrong. That is not the glorious liberty of the children

of God. That is not knowing God in the scriptural
sense.

Take God's way, and then the witnessing Spirit will
come. Of course, people are not assured because they
have *nothing to be assured of!* They have no
salvation, and, therefore, they cannot be assured of it.
Get salvation, and you will get assurance. Oh!
friends. This is what you want. IT IS FOR YOU.
Here it is. There is no other religion recognised in
this Book. All the saints to whom Paul wrote, knew
they were saved. Here and there was an exception,
where they had fallen back and got into bondage, as
some of you have; but, as a rule, he recognises the
fact that they all *were saved,* and were rejoicing in the
assurance of it, and this is the normal condition of the
children of God. I do not say such a person may not
occasionally slip. He may occasionally. He may lose
his scroll, as Pilgrim did, but he cannot, will not rest
till he finds it again!

Then you say, ' I am not to believe, I suppose. '
Oh, yes! you are. Take the blessed record to your
heart, but do not rest in the letter. Do not rest in
the letter. Go ON until you find the *substance* of
things hoped for—the *substance.* There is a substance
in spiritual things quite as much as there is in natural
things, and those who really and truly believe, know
it. No one can testify when you do really and truly
believe but God's Spirit, for the things of a man
knoweth no man save the spirit of a man that is in
him, and just so with the things of God. He searcheth
the hearts and minds, and knows when you are sincere
and real and true; and when you seek Him with all
your heart you will find Him, and He will come and

testify to that fact—and, oh! if you have not this
testimony suspect yourself. Do not throw discredit
upon God. Begin over again and get assurance.

Oh! what POWER assurance of salvation gives!
when the individual can say *I know ;*—not merely *I
believe,* but *I know.* St. John seems to have written
his First Epistle mainly to enable the believers to
know: and ten several times shows how we may
"know" we are saved. Faith is the means to
assurance, but assurance is not faith, and faith is not
assurance. Assurance is the *result* of faith, and when
you have the right sort of faith you will have
assurance. "He that believeth hath the witness in
himself," and until you get assurance do not trust
yourself. Persevere until you get it. God will never
leave a sincere soul in the dark. You must come
down to the foot of the cross in the little children's
way—give up all for Christ, and make up your mind
that you will follow Him at all costs, and then cast
your guilty soul upon His broken, bleeding sacrifice,
and, as soon as you do this, God *will* send the answer
of His Spirit.

But this afternoon I want to go a little farther in
showing how Christ supersedes the Law.

We have noted in a former sermon that He does so,
first, by giving assurance.

Secondly, I want to show that He does so, by giving
POWER OVER SIN. Now we shall be safe here. I
trust this will not be controverted ground. I believe
He can do a great deal more for His people than this,
but we will stop here this afternoon. By-and-bye we
may, perhaps, go farther. *Christ gives His people
power over sin.* Now, this is a necessity of our

position. We have, as we saw last Sunday, been all
slaves of sin. Sin is, indeed, the sting of death.
Now, how is it if there is no deliverance from this
dreadful plague and scourge of God's people—how is
it that the Holy Ghost sets every real child of God
struggling after it ? Whatever may be a man's theory
in his creed, you get him on his knees, and he will
begin to pray to God *to save him from sin.* Sin is
the abominable thing which he hates, and longs to be
delivered from ; and the universal experience of God's
people is that the Spirit urges them to seek to be
saved from *sin.* I have heard people argue powerfully
against the possibility of being delivered from sin,
and the next time I have heard them pray, they have
asked God for the very thing, and I have said, ' Thank
God, that is the Holy Ghost teaching him now; he
cannot help praying for it, whether he believes in it
or not.' If I have been under the power of sin, so as
to become its complete slave, and Jesus Christ comes
and pardons me for the past, and delivers me from
the guilt and condemnation which came upon me in
consequence of the past, what do I want ? I want
some new power. I want something besides pardon.
I want *power* to stand, or I shall be down again the
next minute.

What God does for us through Jesus Christ outside
of us is one thing, and what He does in us by Jesus
Christ is another thing, but the two are simultaneous,
or one so immediately succeeds the other, that we
hardly discern the interval. Now, I say, I want power
to enable me to meet that temptation which is coming
on me to-morrow, as it came on me yesterday, and, if
Jesus Christ pardons me ever so, and leaves me under

the reigning power of my old appetites, what has he done for me? I shall be down in the mud, and to-morrow night I shall be as condemned as ever. I want power. I want regeneration—as the Holy Spirit has put it. I want the *renewing* of the *spirit* of my mind. I want to be created anew in Christ Jesus; " made a new creature."

Now, this is where Jesus Christ transcends the Law. The Law could not renew the spirit of my mind. It could only show me what a guilty rebel I was. It could not put a better spirit in me. It could not extract the venom, but only show it to me, and make me writhe on account of it. But Jesus Christ comes and does this for me—gives me power. How?

Now, I hope those friends who think that I do not sufficiently exalt the Saviour, will mark this. How does He give it to me? *He unites me to Himself.* I am dead to the Law. He delivers me from the condemning power of the Law when He pardons me, and then He does not leave me there, but He "marries" me to Himself. He unites me "to another" husband, and then I attain power to bring forth fruit unto God. A beautiful—a wonderful figure! We may not pursue it; but, oh! what a wonderful figure! Alone under the Law's power, my old husband, I could do nothing but agonise, wrestle, and desire. There was no power in me but when Jesus Christ comes and unites me to Himself; then He gives me power to bring forth fruit unto God. It is by the UNION OF MY SOUL WITH HIM. You say, ' Explain it!' I cannot. God Himself cannot explain it. We cannot explain it, but we *know* it. As Jesus said to Nicodemus:—" The wind bloweth where it listeth, and thou hearest the

sound thereof, but canst not tell whence it cometh,
and whither it goeth: so is every one that is born of
the Spirit." The mystery is too great to be explained,
but there is the beautiful illustration ; united to
Christ I have power to conquer, to subdue, to trample
under foot those things which heretofore have been
my master, and by virtue of Him I retain the power,
and no other way. Oh ! dear friends, what a delusion
there is on the subject of Christian knowledge. If
knowledge could save people, what a wonderful world
we should have to-day.

Knowledge is as powerless as ignorance. A man is
not a whit nearer God, or more like Christ, because he
has his head crammed with this Word. In fact, some
I have known who have been best acquainted with the
Word, who have been the greatest slaves of sin ; and
even ministers of Jesus Christ have confessed to me
that they have been bond slaves of some besetting sin.
The power is not in knowledge—and God is raising up
thousands of witnesses to this fact, that it is not in
knowledge—it is in union with Him, and the little
child in intellect and intelligence, who has the real,
vital, union with Jesus, has more power than the most
cultivated theologian has without Christ. The things
of God can only be understood by those who have the
Spirit of God. The world by wisdom knows not God
any more now, than it did in Paul's days. The things
of the Spirit are only spiritually comprehended.
Hence this beautiful union cannot be explained ; I
only know it is spoken of all through the Bible, both
in the Old Testament and in the New, as *knowing
God.* After God has summed up the failures of His
people, He gives them a promise, and says, "I will

betroth thee unto me in righteousness for ever, and thou shalt KNOW the Lord," as though that were the end of the whole matter, really and truly to know Him. When they come to that living union of soul with Him, it brings the vital sap as it were into the branch of the tree—another of his own beautiful illustrations. " Abide in Me, and I in you. As the branch cannot bear fruit of itself, except it abide in the vine ; no more can ye, except ye abide in Me." You know what the branch is when it is broken off. It is a branch. It retains the form of a branch ; and for a while, the beauty and the greenness of a branch, but it is broken off. There is no power in it. Suppose it could maintain that form. Alas ! human branches often maintain their verdure in a certain beauty, as when first lopped off. But it can never bear fruit. Why ? Because the communication is cut between itself and the vine, and there is no sap in its fibre. Its life is cut off. Now, my friends, you can see why a soul, who has never been truly united to Christ in this living spiritual marriage, cannot bear fruit unto God.

You can be like a branch. You can get so much scriptural knowledge, that you can look just like a real Christian. Alas ! You can get many of the feelings of a Christian, and of the sentiments, as well as a great many of the aspirations and desires, of a Christian. You can be so like a branch that nobody, but Jesus Christ, may know you are not in that true Vine, and yet you have never, as the Apostle says, been grafted on to the olive tree. And, therefore, you go on weeping, and struggling, and trying to perform the function of a living branch, when all the while you are a dead one. You go on trying to bring

7

forth fruit unto God when the one indispensable
condition of fruitfulness is wanting. You have got
every other condition. You may even be nailed up to
the wall close to the vine. You may be such a
professor that nobody may ever doubt you. You may
be so close to the vine that nobody can detect your
want of union, excepting the Gardener who comes and
closely inspects you, and yet you may not have one
fibre truly circulating the real spiritual sap. HENCE
YOU HAVE NO POWER, and down you go when the
temptation comes. Ah! what weary years of strife
some professing Christians have—they would be
ashamed to tell ; death sometimes forces it from
their lips before they die—trying to perform the
functions of living men when they have never been
spiritually made alive. All they have ever had has
been what Paul depicts as the struggle of a poor
convicted sinner unable to bring forth any fruit unto
God.

Now, you say, this union with Him—what is it?
Well, I cannot explain it. You, who know what it is,
cannot explain it—so to know the Lord as to be
conscious of the living sap circulating through your
soul, anointing your eyes with eye-salve, giving you
eyes to see, a voice to speak, feet to run, and hands to
serve—making you in all respects a " new creature."

Now, my dear friends, those of you who have not
experienced this, never mind who comes to you and
brings a Bible, and says, ' Do you believe this and
that ? if you do you are saved.' Say, ' Miserable
comforters are ye all : I will never be content until I
know God.'

I made up my mind to this when I was 15 years of

age. I had had the strivings of God's Spirit all my life, since I was about two years old. My dear mother has often told me how she went upstairs to find me crying, and when she questioned me, I said I was crying, because I had sinned against God. Thank the Lord, I do not say this boastingly I have good cause to be ashamed that I was so long before I fully gave myself up; but all through my childhood I was graciously sheltered by a watchful mother from outward sin, and, in fact, brought up as a Christian. When I came to be between 15 and 16, when, I believe, I was thoroughly converted, the great temptation of Satan to me was this : ' You must not expect such a change as you read of in books. You have been half a Christian all your life. You always feared God. You must content yourself with this.' Oh! how I was frightened ! It must have been the Spirit of God that taught me. I was frightened at it. I said, ' No, no. ' My heart is as bad as other people's and if I have not sinned outwardly I have inwardly. I cried to God to show me the evil of my heart, and said, ' I will never rest till I am as thoroughly and truly changed, and know it, as any thief, or any great outward sinner.' I went on seeking God in this way for six weeks, often till two o'clock in the morning, wrestling, and I told the Lord I would never give up, if I died in the search, until I found God, and I did find Him, as every soul does, when it comes to him in that way. I cried for nothing on earth or in heaven, but that I might find Him, whom my soul panted after, and I did find Him, and you can find Him. I knew Him. I can't tell how, but I knew Him. I knew He was well pleased with me. I knew that we held sweet converse often to the small hours of the morning together, and I know that I was as happy in His love, and far more happy than I ever was in any human love before or since.

Now, friends, you can all have this union. He is no respecter of persons. He has bought it for us. He saw our weakness. He contemplated our moral inability. He need not have come if we could have known God by the Law. If that old covenant had been perfect, there would have been no room for a second. It brought us not into the full realisation and enjoyment of God, but the new covenant does. It cleanses the conscience from dead works to serve the living God, and God is henceforth revealed to His people, and they walk with Him. "If a man love Me, he will keep My words ; and My Father will love him, and We will come unto him and make Our abode with him." And when a man has got the Father and the Son, he is a match for Satan and all his forces. Union with Christ!

Oh! do you think this is a mere allegory of the Apostle's? It is a beautiful illustration. When He delivers us from the condemning, reigning power of the Law, we become married to Jesus Christ. Then we get a power to produce, in our affections, and hearts, and lives, and all about us, such things as God delights in.

Now, mark, all through the New Testament, and, indeed, the Bible, no truth is taught with greater force and frequency than this, that without a vital union of soul with Christ, all ceremonies, creeds, beliefs, professions, church ordinances, are sounding brass and tinkling cymbals, and all who trust in them

will be deceived. This is the very essence of the
Gospel. This is what He came for and (oh! how my
heart bleeds to think and say it) all who do not
attain to this real vital union with Him, will be *lost.*
Everything else falls short of our need and the purpose
and end of the Gospel of Christ. He came on purpose
for us to have this union with Himself. Neither
circumcision, nor uncircumcision, nor anything else
availeth anything, but this faith, which worketh by
love, and brings the Spirit of Christ into our hearts.
Oh! bear with me; dear friends, have you got it?
Have you got this vital union with Christ? Are you
bringing forth fruit unto God? If not, I beseech you
give up daubing yourselves with untempered mortar,
and trying to make yourselves believe you are right,
when you are all wrong. However much desire,
purpose, hope, aspiration, struggle, or whatever else
you have, if you have not attained to this, you are not
saved yet, and you are not in the kingdom.

In conclusion, "bring forth fruit unto God," or, as
the Apostle has it, "having your fruit unto holiness and
the end everlasting life"—and in another place, for
the "end of the commandment," the purpose of
the commandment, the ultimatum of the commandment, "is charity," love, "out of a pure heart," and
so in many other passages; but we just take these at
random.

The result! What is the result? "That we may
bring forth fruit unto God." Jesus Christ in this
union recognises the fact that we are still in the body;
still in the world; and that we are open to the attacks
of Satan. He knows—has foreseen, and has provided
for, the temptations of the flesh, that is, the temptations

which come to us through our natural appetites, and instincts, and desires, as they came to Him. He was hungry after enduring the great temptation in the wilderness. There was no sin in being hungry. He was intensely hungry, for He had nerves, and a brain, and a heart, as we have. He was a perfect man, and he suffered all the consequences of that lengthened strain upon His nervous system, and the Devil took advantage of the existence of that intensely excited condition of His body by tempting Him unlawfully to gratify it. For he said, " Command these stones that they be made bread." This was unlawful under the circumstances, (we will not stop now to enquire why—) and, therefore, He said, " Get thee behind me, Satan." He would rather suffer the hunger, than unlawfully gratify it, and, therefore, He did not commit sin. It matters not (and this will meet the case of some who have written to me) how intensely excited any physical appetite may be —*that is not sin.* The more you suffer through the excitement of the physical appetite, of whatever kind it may be, the more Jesus Christ sympathises with you, for He was tempted in all points, like as we are, yet without sin ; and if you endure temptation, He will sympathise with you, more than with the man who does not have to endure and resist. You do not sin because of the appetite merely being excited. I think Satan gets some sincere souls to bring themselves into condemnation, when God does not condemn them. If you resist as He did ;—if you say, " Get thee behind me, Satan,"—you sin not. What was Eve's sin? Unlawful self-gratification. The Devil might have tempted her until now, if she had lived so long; but if she had steadily resisted him, she would not have brought sin into the world.

Under the Law you see that it is sin, and you struggle against it, but you have no power to resist, and down you go. United to Christ you see that it is sin, and you have power to resist, and you resist it, and the Devil runs away ; and that is the difference. You are married to a new husband now, and He is more than a match for the old Devil. He is a conquered foe, while you abide in Christ. He can torment, harass, and excite you, and stimulate your natural appetites, but he cannot make you sin, while you abide in Christ. " He that is begotten of God keepeth himself and that Wicked One toucheth him not." " Ye are strong and have overcome the Wicked One."

Then, again, we are open to the temptations of the world, but this is provided for. Jesus Christ knows that we are susceptible to the liking of nice things like other people, and great things, and ambitious schemes, and the world's praises and censures. God's people are only sadly too familiar with this, and the weak part of their nature would respond to it, and they would fall ; but now they are united to Christ, and He opens their eyes to see that it is Satan and the world. When the Devil takes them to the top of the pinnacle, and shows them all the glory of the world, he tries to make them think it would be very nice to have it ; he tempts them to think it hard that they should be regarded as such paltry and mean people, because they belong to Christ ; but when they are thoroughly and truly united to Jesus, He gives them power to say as He did, " Get thee behind me, Satan," for it is written, " Thou shalt love the Lord thy God, and Him ONLY shalt thou serve "—not Him and the world. Oh ! thank God, if you have got there. Praise the Lord, if you understand that.

Then he comes not only through these avenues, but he comes again with direct, subtle, spiritual influence, with his old insinuation, as he came to Eve, and says, " Hath God said " this, or that ? He tries to inject doubts as to God's goodness and veracity into the believer's soul, as he used to do under the Law, and under the Law the convicted sinner's soul used to swell with rebellion, and say, ' Yes, it is hard and cruel.'

Now, Satan still comes and vomits these thoughts, and tries to excite these ill-feelings and these chargings of God foolishly in the believer's soul, but by virtue of his union with Christ, who came not to do His own will, but His Father's, and who spoke only the things that His Father bade Him, the believer says, " Though He slay me, yet will I trust in Him." "Shall not the Judge of all the earth do right?"—and the Devil is gone. And then when the Devil is foiled at all these points, he tries higher ground. ' Really you ' are a wonderful Christian—you are. You have had ' special grace, for surely very few people can have ' resisted the amount of temptation that you have. ' Really you must be one of God's specially favoured ' ones. Now cast yourself down. It is written, " He ' " shall give His angels charge concerning you.' ' Spiritual presumption next. When he is foiled through the world, and the flesh, and the Devil, and then he doffs his old robe and comes as an angel of light. But the soul's Bridegroom is hard by, and he says ' Be not ignorant of Satan's devices. Behold I am thy salvation. Trust and be not afraid.' And so the soul refuses to cast itself into unnecessary troubles, and is content to abide in, and walk with its Lord. That is how He gives us the victory. He shows us Satan's devices, and gives us power. I cannot tell you how. We don't know how. We only know that He gives it to us, and we only know that if one instant separated from Him we fall and become as other men. We only know that in these seasons when our faith has relaxed its grasp, we have gone down in the mud and been overcome as others. It is by faith we stand, and while, like Peter, we keep our eye on Him, and hold Him fast, the waves may roar, and the winds may howl, but He holds us by virtue of this union, and we bring forth fruit unto God. We have power over the Devil. He said, " I will give you power over all the power of the enemy." This *is the deliverance of the* SAINTS. This is the life of the *saints.* This is the *fight of faith.* THIS IS THE JOY OF SALVATION. This is the SORT OF RELIGION THAT DOES TO DIE WITH ! ! !

People all over the land are astounded at our poor, weak, illiterate, Salvation Army Soldiers. A gentleman, in a meeting on Easter Monday, a leading man of thought and experience in the holiness world, who was there all day—when my daughter said, ' Why don't you speak ? '—said, ' One feels as if one can't speak in these meetings.' ' Why ? ' These people have such unction from the Holy One that they are wiser than their teachers. Another gentleman, of considerable position, too, in the religious world, said, ' I feel like getting down at their feet. I feel as if they could teach me.' How is it that they have such

power—these babes in intellect and intelligence? All
over the land people say this to me. People who talk
and go ahead in other meetings, when they get into
our meetings, say, ' I can't. They are so far ahead of
me that, to tell you the truth, I have nothing to say.'
I say, the Lord have mercy upon you, and make haste
and come up after them. Only get down from your
high mightiness as low as these people, and you will
get it. It is not *because* they are poor and illiterate,
that they have power, but because they are babes in
spirit. Even as Christ said, " I thank thee, oh ! Father,
that Thou hast hid these things from the wise and
prudent, and hast revealed them unto babes." The
simple spirit, the teachable believing soul—oh ! how
much more it learns of God, in one hour's precious
communion, than Doctors of Divinity learn in weeks of
close study, who have not got it, because it is the
SPIRIT that teaches the things of God. This is union
with Jesus that bringeth forth fruit unto God, and, oh !
the wonderful things it enables us to bring forth. If
you would all follow me, as far as I have gone this
afternoon, and make the resolution I made at 15 years
of age, not to be put off with theories, but that you
will KNOW THE LORD, that you *will* have this Divine
union, and that you *will* never rest till you get it and
know you have it—if we could all get thus far by next
Sunday—what happiness there would be amongst you.
There *would* be some Hallelujahs. Many of you would
be surprised, how you would find your tongues. A
gentleman once said to me ' I never did shout in my
life, but upon my word I couldn't help it.' I said,
' Amen. It's time, then, you began.' I hope it may
be the same with many of you. When the Lord comes

to His Temple and fills it with His glory, you won't know what to do. You must find vent somewhere, or you will be as the poor old negro said he was—" Ready to bust his waistcoat." We feel so about temporal things. People drop down dead with joy. People shriek with grief. People's hearts stand still with wonder at the news they have heard, perhaps from some prodigal boy. I heard of a mother, not long ago, whom some one injudiciously told of the sudden return of her son, who dropped down dead, and never spoke. And when the Master comes to His Temple, that glorious blessed Holy Saviour, whom you profess so to long after and to love, and who has been absent so many years, and whom you have been seeking after with strong crying and tears, when He comes, do you think it will be too much to shout your song, or go on your face, or do any extravagant thing? Oh! no, if there is reality, you cannot help yourself. The mani- festation will be according to your nature. One will fall down and weep in quietness, and the other will get up and shout and jump. You cannot help it. I have read of two martyrs one of whom rejoiced in the realisation of God's presence, and the other was in darkness, yet did not deny his Lord. He continued in the way of obedience, and the other was encouraging him to hope and believe that the Master would come ; but He had not come, when they started from the dungeon to the stake ; so they fixed upon a sign, and the or e said to the other, " If He comes, you will give me the sign on the road." The Master did come, but the martyr could not confine himself to the sign. He shouted, raising his arms to his fellow-martyr, "He's come, He's come, He's come." He couldn't help it.

When He comes you won't be ashamed who knows it. When you really get a living Christ for your husband, you will be prouder than the bride, you will have got a husband worth being proud of, and you will love to acknowledge and praise Him, and the day is coming when you will crown Him before all the host of heaven. The Lord help you to accept Him, and put away everything that hinders His coming.   Amen.

THE FRUITS OF UNION
WITH CHRIST.

THE FRUITS OF UNION WITH CHRIST.

ROMANS, viii. 1-4 —" *That the righteousness of the law might be fulfilled in us, who walk not after the flesh, but after the Spirit.*"

WE dealt, on Sunday week, with " What the Law could not do ; " and last Sabbath afternoon we dealt with " What Jesus Christ could do," by uniting us with Himself and giving us power. I want, this afternoon, to direct your attention to the *fruits* of this union— THE LAW FULFILLED IN US. What does it mean ?

First.—I want just to say two or three words about Law in the abstract. There seems to me to be an awful misconception of the Apostle's writings respecting the Law, caused by " wresting " and misapplying what he says on justification by faith. People should bear in mind that much of this Epistle, and some others, was written on purpose to meet the extreme legal notions of the Jews, who had no other idea of righteousness than that of their own efforts to keep the Law (*Romans* x. 3), and that, therefore, the Apostle was bound, as any other writer would be in such circumstances, to put the extreme view on the other side. Many, not considering this, separate these passages from their explanatory connections, and from all the rest of the Word of God, and preach, now a-days, that we have nothing to do with the Law. Hence, there has come to be a spirit of Antinomianism abroad in the land, compared with which the Anti-nomianism of bygone ages was harmless. God helping me, I shall never cease to lift up my voice against it.

Now please, *first* note that there is in this writing,
talking, and singing about the ~~Law~~ a great deal of
mental fog and confusion. People should be very
careful, when they come to such matters as these, to
be clear in their own minds, as to what the Apostle is
writing about; but I find frequently in such writings
and songs a total misapprehension as to the meaning
of the Apostle, and a total confounding of the Moral
with the Ceremonial Law. Now, always mind, when
you read anything about the Law, to examine and
find out which Law is meant, whether it is the great
Moral Law, which never has been, and never can be,
abrogated, or the Ceremonial Law, which in Christ,
confessedly was done away. Mind which, because your
salvation may depend upon that point. If you make
a mistake there, you may be lost through it; therefore,
be, very careful. Now, I say that people confound
these, and, consequently, there is a perfect hotch-
potch of theology in this day, which I defy anybody
to understand. People do not know what they are
to believe, or what they are not to believe. As a
gentleman said, not long ago, 'it is confusion
confounded. I go to one meeting and hear this, and
then I go to another meeting and hear that, and, very
often, in the very same meeting, the speakers will get
up and flatly contradict each other!' 'Exactly' I
said, 'but you have got the Bible. Why don't you
study that for yourself? Why not use your own
common sense—why not let your conscience speak?'
'But,' said he, 'why do not our ministers do it?'
'Because,' said I, 'many of them do not know it
themselves. Let your conscience speak, and God will
not let you go wrong' It is an honest heart people

want, and then they will get the light. People sing about the Law, talk about the Law, and glory in being free from the Law, in a lawless, Antinomian spirit, as far from anything Paul ever wrote or meant, as hell is from heaven! Oh, it is an awfully bad sign, when people are out of love with the Law of God! David made his boast in the Law of his God, he meditated on it by day and by night, and its precepts were his delight; he loved it with all his soul, and so did David's Son, and He is too much in love with His Father's Law and Will, to hold fellowship with anybody who does not love it. As He said to the Jews, "He that is of God, heareth *God's words*; ye, therefore, hear them not, because ye are not of God;" and, again, of His disciples, "For I have given unto them the *words* which Thou gavest me." So, mind, if you do not love the *words*, the expression of the *will* of God, you do not love God, and if you do not love the Father, neither do you love the Son. This is the very accusation which He brought against the Jews, that they had made void His Father's Law. Let us mind, then, the distinction always made between the great Moral and the Ceremonial Law.

In the second place: I want you to note, that when you have ascertained that the Apostle is speaking of the Moral Law—and he appears to speak disparagingly of it—he is always referring to its inability to justify a sinner, or to produce spiritual life. This, he says, it could not do; but he never speaks disparagingly of it as the guide and *standard* of spiritual life, after life *is* given. No! he goes back to it as the only standard, and so did Jesus Christ. They continually refer to the Law as the highest expression of the holiness and

righteousness of God, and as the standard by which we
are to set our souls and consciences. What other
standard have we but the Law? How am I to judge
of my thoughts, words, and actions but by the Law?
Where has Jesus Christ given me any other gauge?
And if people would *but read on*, and let the Apostle
explain himself, they would understand him better,
and not get into such tanglements and mazes! Paul
is most careful to guard himself against the Antinomian
conclusions which he saw *might* be drawn from isolated
parts of his writings. He says, "Do we, then, make
void the Law through faith? nay, we establish the
Law." And, again, "Wherefore the Law is holy, and
the commandment holy, just, and good;" and, again,
when he says, that "To them that are without Law He
became as without Law;" he guards himself by a
parenthesis, "Being not without Law to God, but
under the Law to Christ." That is under the great
universal Law of love, which fulfils all other law; for
"Love is the fulfilling of the Law." Love is the very
spirit and essence of the Law. The Law is to me the
highest expression of what I OUGHT to be, in my
relations to my Creator and in my relations to my
fellow-creatures. Now, can what *ought to be* ever
be abrogated? Does it stand to sense? Can the
rightness of things ever be altered? Can God ever
make two and two five, and can God make evil
good and good evil? He can make an evil *person*
good, by saving him from the evil and making him
good; but God cannot make evil itself good, and good
evil, and He never professes to do it.

Oh, this confounding of things! how it does ruin
and befog poor souls; How can it ever be less the

duty of the creature to love and serve the Creator, than it was when he first came pure and spotless from His hand? How can it ever be less my duty to love my neighbour as myself, than it was at the beginning, or how can I satisfy my conscience with less than loving all men with a pure, benevolent love such as God bears to them, in my measure and according to my capacity? The same standard remains, and the difference between God's scheme of salvation and the scheme of salvation so widely preached now, is that man's scheme proposes to get me into heaven without fulfilling this Law, while God's scheme proposes to give me power to FULFIL IT. Alas! I am afraid many will not find out which is the right one, man's or God's till they get to the Judgment Seat and find it out too late!

Now, I say, that there is not a word, rightly understood and interpreted by correlative Scriptures, in the whole New Testament that disparages or ignores or sets aside the Law of God—not a word! Do you think the Apostle was as unphilosophical as many now-a-days? Did he not know what he wrote? Is he not as clear as a bell? And now he comes to the climax of his argument, the great end and purpose towards which he has been advancing in his preceding reasonings: "THAT the righteousness of the Law might be FULFILLED in us." As though he had said, "This great and glorious end which was lost in Adam shall be re-found and restored." So the old serpent shall be circumvented at last, and God's people shall be able to fulfil this beautiful ideal of rectitude and righteousness which God has planned for man—Jesus Christ shall destroy the work of the devil, restore man, and enable him to walk in the light, even as He is in the light. *What the Law tried to do by a restraining power from without, the Gospel does by an inspiring power from within. That* is the difference. I could not keep it in the letter, but, united to my heavenly Bridegroom, I can keep it in the Spirit. He fills me with His love, and this enables me to keep the Law, for love is the fulfilling of the Law. "Love worketh no ill to his neighbour" of any kind, and, again, the great Teacher said, "For *all* the Law is fulfilled in one word—Thou shalt love thy neighbour as thyself." If you do that, will you injure your neighbour? See how the Spirit fulfills the Law! If you love your neighbour, will you misrepresent him, cheat him, envy him anything that he possesses or enjoys? 'No,' you say, 'of course not; it is a contradiction.' Very well, then, get this love in your soul and you will fulfil the Law. Love is the fulfilling of the Law, and he that loveth in this sense dwelleth in God and God in him. Love is the fulfilling of the Law, and the great glory of the Gospel of Christ is that it brings us back to love His Law, and, as the angels delight in it, and, as all holy intelligences delight in it, so we delight in it, and the righteousness of the Law—high, deep, and broad, and long as it is—shall be fulfilled in us, "who walk not after the flesh, but after the Spirit."

Then, I say, the Apostle evidently considered this fulfilment of the Law of Righteousness in us as the highest end of our existence and of redemption; for, he says, God sent His Son that the righteousness of the Law may be fulfilled in us. Mark, *not* that its claims shall be abated: Oh! not one jot or tittle shall ever be abated. They cannot. God could not abate them. Not that the righteousness of the Law shall cease to have a claim upon *you*. Oh! if He could have saved us like that, Christ need not have come at all. He could have saved us without a Mediator. No, no! but that the righteousness of the Law may be FULFILLED in us as it was in Him. That we should be brought to the full stature of men and women in Christ Jesus, that we should have this spirit of our heavenly Bridegroom, by which we fulfil the *law* and the servant, in his measure, shall be as his Lord.

How? As I explained, last Sunday, *first:* We shall be delivered from the reigning, condemning power of the Law by virtue of an infinite, vicarious sacrifice punished in our stead, and then, married to Him, we shall *serve* in the newness of the Spirit, and not in the oldness of the letter.

I want to be eminently and intensely practical, for the sake of the hungering and thirsting souls who are asking me in their letters, 'Tell me how? Help me?'

Just let us look at this result (in fourth verse). People talk about glorifying Christ; but, it seems to me, this does glorify Him. It seems to me here is something to glory in, that He has circumvented the old serpent and snatched the prey from his teeth, and restored it, and enabled man, after all, to fulfil the righteousness of God. Not only in what Christ does for us; but what He does IN US, that God should look on you and say, ' I am well pleased. There is nothing there contrary to my will.' He will give you the testimony, as He did Enoch, that your ways please Him, that your thoughts please Him, that your motives, and purposes and desires, and actions

please Him.   That is what the Gospel proposes to do.
We have seen how this spirit is produced.   Now
let us look at the fruits, and first :—

This fruit is brought forth in THE AFFECTIONS!

Those people who are thus united to Christ fulfil the
Law in their affections.   You know it is commonly
said that if you get hold of the affections of a man or a
woman you get hold of him or her.   So you do.   This
is the touchstone, and there is nothing in which I have
been so grieved and disappointed as in the manifest
want of quickness, livingness in the affections of God's
people for Him.   Oh! how I have seen this come out.
The coldness, the unsympathetic character of a great
many people's religion, and yet people whom one would
not like to unchristianise.   I cannot explain it by any
better term than want of *quickness.*   I have often been
struck with the difference when you touch individuals
on some point that affects them personally, and on those
which relate to the Kingdom of God, and have been
tempted to say with the Apostle, " All men seek their
own, and not the things that are Jesus Christ's."   Alas!
I fear it is very largely so.   You talk with a lady about
the salvation of her children's souls, the souls of her
neighbours, and her servants, or about the cause of God
in general, and she will talk " good " with you, so to
speak, and you will feel, ' yes, it is all very well,' but it
doesn't seem to come up from the depths.   It seems to
come from the throat, so to speak ; a sort of superficial,
surface kind of thing.   But, if a child is dangerously
ill, how quick the mother's sympathies, how ready to
listen, how willing to do anything that you suggest to
help the child.   If the business is in danger, if a man
has got into difficulties and you can suggest any plan

by which he may get out of them, how quickly his attention is aroused. His interest doesn't flag, because the subject touches him to the quick. It is *his* concern, and just so in many other things. God forbid I should judge all Christians. No, no, no!—there are blessed exceptions. There are many like David—rivers of water do run down their eyes; but I am speaking of the mass of professors. I am afraid, that in their affections there is a great deal of this lukewarm superficiality. Why is it? Because such people do not abide in Christ, if ever they were in Him. They do not keep the freshness and the quickness of the Spirit of Jesus. They do not give themselves time to do it for one thing, or care about it for another. We want the constant indwelling of the Holy Spirit to quicken our spiritual perceptions and keep us awake. It is Satan's great desire to rock us to sleep, and there is no quality in which the disciples have been more conspicuous than in going to sleep since the time when the professed watchers went to sleep in the garden; but Jesus, in his mercy and love, is always wakening them. But, oh! this disposition to go to sleep, to lose our quickness of perception. Now, friends, what must you do? You must do as you did at first. Cry and believe till your soul is filled with the love of God.

I shall never forget reading, when only fourteen years of age, a sentiment of a precious and valiant soldier of the Lord Jesus, who is now in glory. Speaking of putting a test, he said that people might easily find out whether they loved God or themselves best:—"Suppose you were in business in a little village, and were doing pretty well, and everything was going smoothly with you; but there was nothing for you to

do there for the Kingdom of God, no particular way in
which you could serve or glorify God; and, suppose
there was another little village hard by, where there
was nothing whatever doing for the Kingdom, and you
felt it laid upon your soul to go there in order that you
might preach to unconverted people and raise a church,
and do something for souls. Ah! but you have got a
nice business and you don't know whether you would
prosper or not in the other village. Now you may know
whether you are serving God or yourself first, by this
test. If you are seeking God, you will be ready to go
to that strange village and trust Him with the consequences; but, if you are serving yourself, you will
stop where you are. The Lord has helped me to apply
that many a time to many things besides business, and
to keep the Kingdom of God FIRST, as I made up my
mind it should be first always—not in time merely, but
in degree—all the way through. If I love Him best, I
shall feel for Him deepest, and shall act for Him first.
If I love Him best, I shall feel for Him more deeply than
for my husband or children, near and precious as they are
and dearer than my own life a thousand times; but
He will be dearer still and His interests; and if, as
Jesus Christ says, His interests require me to sacrifice
these precious and beloved ones of my soul, then I
shall sacrifice them; for the philosophical reason that
I love Him better than I love them, and, therefore, I
shall lay them on His altar, to promote His glory. If
I understand it, this is the fruit of the Spirit in the
affections—God first. I am afraid, in a great many
instances, it is husband first, wife first, children first,
and, I am afraid, in some cases, business first, and then
God may take what there is left and be thankful for

that! Now, if you are in this condition you need not
expect joy, peace, power. You will never get it if you
do. God will have to make you over again before you
can get it, and to alter the conditions of His salvation.
Oh! but if you will lay it all on His altar, that is quite
another thing.

As I said to a lady, a little time ago, ' The Lord can
take your husband, if you refuse to *give* him to Him ; '
and I am afraid God's people often compel Him to
take their darlings, because they make them idols;
whereas, if they had laid them on His altar, they
might have had them back, as Abraham received back
Isaac. I said to a gentleman, ' Mind that God does not
burn down your barns, wreck your ships, and take
away your riches God loves your soul enough to do
it, if you let these things prevent that whole-hearted
consecration which He requires.' We are in His
hands. "Whom He loveth He chasteneth," and if
you want to keep the precious things you have, oh !
put them at His feet, and hold them in subordination
to Him. First, in your affections! He is a jealous
God, and jealousy in God is very much like jealousy
in us. It is the same characteristic of mind, only
. purified from selfishness. He is a jealous God, and if
you will love these things better than Him, and if you
will not give Him your affections, then He will chastise
you, or—what is worse still—He will take His Holy
Spirit from you.

Fruit in your affections. Oh, if Christ had your
affections, how it would operate in everything ! The
wife would not be always grumbling because the
husband had to go out three or four evenings a week
on the Lord's errands—only let them be the Lord's

errands. The husband would not grudge to give his wife up to go to help to win souls, because it deprived him of her society or a few comforts that she might provide for him if she were near. The parents would not grudge to restrain their children as Eli did. He did not restrain them from that which they liked, and you know the fruit it brought. Parents who love God best will not allow their children to learn anything which could not be pressed into the service of God. They will not allow them to run with the giddy multitude, to dance or do anything the devil might inspire them to desire. "No!" they will say, "my children belong to God, and I am going to train them for God and God only." Bless the Lord, He helped me to make up my mind to do that before I became a mother; and He has helped me to keep that promise (though I have not been as faithful to it as I ought), casting aside resolutely every temptation to the contrary. And now He is giving me the fruit of my self-denial in the souls and labours of my precious children. One after another, as they grow up, they take their natural place in the temple of the Lord, and I believe they shall go out no more for ever. Oh, that parents would do it! Parents *might* save their children. I know what a mother's feelings are. I know the temptation there is to see them shine in competition with others, and to excel others. I know it all; but I said, 'No; "Get thee behind me, Satan." I will keep them *for God;*' and He has enabled me to keep them for Him. Bless His holy name!

I loved Him better than I loved them, and, much as I loved them (and those who know me know I *do* love them), I would see them all in a row laid in their coffins before I would sacrifice His interests and lose their souls. Do you love Him best? Test yourself. Do you love Him more than all else? Are you holding everything in subordination to Him?

Further, this fruit will come out in our members— our bodies; and oh! there is a deep spiritual meaning which, I trust, many of you know, in those words of the Apostle, "The body is dead because of sin;" but " He shall quicken your mortal bodies by His Spirit, that dwelleth in you" It is killed to the Devil, as well as to sin, and all the uses of Satan; but it is quickened by the Spirit for the use of God, so that you can render not only the calves of your lips, but your hands, and eyes, and brain, and heart, and feet, and the whole of your body to Him—your members instruments of righteousness unto God. Hence, such a person will not feel his eyes are his own, to rove at random wherever he lists. Such a person will not feel his tongue is his own, to speak as he pleases. He will " bridle it," as James says, when tempted to speak unadvisedly. Such a person will not feel that his hands are his own, to waste the time, in which he ought to be doing something for God. Such a person will not feel his feet his own, to carry him where he likes, but where his Master would have him go—his whole body consecrated, and, especially, his *tongue*— consecrated to God, to testify for Him. He will feel that he must feed his body, as my husband often says, on the same principle that a man feeds his horse— to keep it in the best working condition for God— never eating anything that will bring the devils of dyspepsia dancing round his soul. And, not only so, with eating and drinking, but all his surroundings and deportment must be in keeping. It is the *Lord's body*; and, if you love Him best, you will keep it for Him: as the bride and the bridegroom keep themselves for each other, so you will keep it for Him.

This fruit will also appear in our family relations. We shall fulfil the Law to our neighbours. You see, God wants only what we have to give Him. He is not a hard master reaping where He has not sown, and the Great Teacher said, "This is the first and great commandment," embracing all the rest, "Thou shalt love the Lord thy God with all thy heart, and mind, and soul, and strength," and the second is like unto it, "And thy neighbour as thyself;" and the man who does these is a perfect man, and fulfils the law; and when you have the fulness of love that enables you to love God best and your neighbour as yourself—enables you to do for the souls and bodies of your fellows what you would like that they should do for you, if you changed places, then the Law is fulfilled in you. Such people cannot sit 365 days in the year at the table with unconverted people, and never try to get them saved. Such people cannot abide in the same house with unbelievers, and not make them miserable. Oh, no. The unconverted say, ' It's too wretched to live here. I must get out of this crying and praying for me all day long.' As a servant once said, she couldn't stand it. She had had praying enough at home, without coming there to have it. She did stand it for six weeks, and broke down at the family altar and GOT SAVED, and became a preacher afterwards. This spirit of love will make every unconverted sinner within your reach so miserable that they will have to be converted or run

away. How would you do if they were DYING? You
would run about in every direction to get a minister.
What a pity you did not feel like this twelve years ago.
You might have got the sinner converted then, and
he have been serving the Lord all the time? But, now
he is dying, what a stir you make What a purely
selfish religion that is. You want him saved, so that
he may get *into* HEAVEN, not that he might serve,
honour, and glorify God. You don't care at all about
that. He might live on in disobedience. Oh, be as
much concerned for the honour of God as you are for
your friend's salvation at the last, and then God will
know how to save them.

This fruit will also appear in your church relations.
It will bring forth fruit. As the Apostle says,
"Exhorting one another daily," not suffering sin in
your neighbour; reproving each other, and "confessing
your faults one to the other." Where is any of it
done? I should like very much to attend such a
meeting, if you invite me, where Christians really and
honestly confess their faults one to the other, and
pray for one another, beseeching the Lord to heal
them in those particular points where they have
failed, telling one another of the deep things of God
and talkingly lovingly and freely to one another as
they used to do. It is part of the communion of
saints—"exhort one another daily." The devil is at
work daily. The world is plying for us daily. The
flesh is pleading daily. Everything evil goes on
daily. Why should not this exhorting one another,
confessing your faults to one another, and praying for
one another go on daily too?

Is it a fact that we are each other's keeper? Is it a fact that God will require for our influence over other souls? I believe it.

Then in our relations to the world——. But I forestalled this in my address on " Aggressive Effort." And now let us go down on our knees before God and ask Him to work this love in us, and give us this spirit, that we may thus FULFIL THIS LAW in all its relations.

WITNESSING FOR CHRIST.

WITNESSING FOR CHRIST.

Acts i. 8 (latter clause).—" *Ye shall be witnesses unto me both in Jerusalem, and in all Judæa, and in Samaria, and unto the uttermost parts of the earth.*"

Acts v. 32.—" *And ye are His witnesses of these things*"

AGAIN and again the same vocation and commission is bestowed upon the apostles and disciples. To the ends of the earth and to the end of time this commission comes down to every one of the Lord's own, for He says :—" Go ye into all the world and preach the Gospel to every creature ; and, lo, I am with you always, even unto the end of the world." That embraces us. And to every disciple who has preceded, or is to follow us, is promised His Divine Presence in this glorious work of testifying for Him.

God needs witnesses in this world.

Why ? Because the whole world is in revolt against Him. The world has gone away from God. The world ignores God, denies and contradicts His testimony, misunderstands His character, government, and purposes, and is gone off into utter and universal revolt and rebellion. Now if God is to keep any hold upon man at all, and have any influence with him, He must be represented down here. There was no other way of doing it. If a province of this realm were in anarchy and rebellion, unless there be some persons in the province whose duty it is to represent the Queen and her Government, it will lapse altogether and be

9

lost to the kingdom for ever. So God must be represented, and, praise His name, He has had His faithful witnesses from the beginning until now. As the Apostle says—"He left not Himself without witness." Down from the days of Enoch, who walked with God, to this present hour, God has always had His true and faithful witnesses. In the worst times there have been some burning and shining lights. Sometimes few and far between, sometimes, like Noah, one solitary man in a whole generation of men, witnessing for God—but one, at least, there *has been.* God has not left Himself without witness.

But Jesus Christ the Son—the well-beloved of the Father—He was *the great witness.* He came especially to manifest, to testify of, and to reveal the Father to men. This was His great work. He came not to testify of Himself, but of His Father, not to speak His own words, but the words His Father gave Him to speak. He came to reveal God to men. He was *the* "Faithful and True Witness." And when He had to leave the world and go back to His Father, then He commissioned His disciples to take His place, and to be God's witnesses on earth. And Oh! friends, God's *real people* are His *only* witnesses. He will not allow angels—we do not know why—to witness for Him here. He has called man to witness for Him,—His people—" Ye shall be witnesses unto Me."

Jesus " witnessed a good confession," did he not? He witnessed nobly, consistently, bravely, of His Father, and sealed His testimony with His blood. The world treated Him as it has treated most of God's faithful witnesses from the beginning; it persecuted Him; it slew Him, as it *would* every faithful witness f.1 God -if God allowed it—and would leave itself without a single spiritual light: for the spirit that worketh in the children of disobedience hath an eternal and devilish hatred of every real, living, spiritual child of God. It hates him as it hated the Son Himself, and it is not the Devil's fault if he does not extinguish and exterminate every such witness. It is because God will not allow him, but holds us, keeps us, saves us, in spite of him.

The Lord commissioned, then, His disciples to be His witnesses, and He said—oh! beautiful words, and yet, how much they involve which few understand— " As Thou hast sent Me into the world, even so send I them into the world " *Even so :* as Thou hast sent Me to be Thy representative in the world, to spend and be spent for Thee, and shed My blood for Thee, if necessary, so send I them ;—and so He did send them, and they had just the same fare as their Master, and many of them just the same end. But they were faithful witnesses, and they went forward and testified everywhere, to the Jews and to the Gentiles, in the Temple and in the Market Place, by the wayside and in the highways and hedges—they went and testified of this Saviour, and charged the wicked Jews with His crucifixion, and God accompanied their testimony by the Spirit, and thousands upon thousands were converted—turned from their rebellion to God.

Now, the fact that witnessing is necessary shows that *there is controversy going on in the world* as to the things and claims of God—that there are two sides to this. The great mass of mankind say, that God's truth is a lie. They say it virtually, if they do not say it in words ; and many thousands of them, alas ! in words, also. They deny, many of them, His very existence, and say there is neither Heaven nor Hell—that Jesus Christ was a mere man—that religion is a myth, and that there is no such thing as the knowledge of forgiveness of sins—that this witnessing is a grand delusion of the imagination, and nothing further.

Now, Christ calls His people to go and be witnesses to these facts. Witnesses, you know, must deal with facts, not theories—not what they merely think, or suppose, or have heard, but what they *know*. Now God wants His people to witness to facts—to something that has been done, and is being done—something that is and continues to be—fact.

And He wants us to be GOOD witnesses, too. Oh! how much depends upon the character of a witness even in an earthly court. If you can cast a reflection upon the character or the veracity of a witness, you shake his testimony, and take away its value. Oh! how important that Christ's witnesses should be good witnesses—that is, that they should fairly and truly represent Him and His truth—for, if they misrepresent Him, somebody is sure to be damned through their inconsistency—and, how awful to have the blood of souls upon our skirts! To misrepresent a man, or woman, or child, is bad enough, but to misrepresent God!—to show a caricature of the religion of Jesus Christ!—to live a wrong life and still profess to be a Christian, saying to people, virtually, "Look at me :— the way I live and act—WHAT I AM—this is the religion of Jesus Christ." I say, such a man had far better have a millstone hanged about his neck and be drowned in the depths of the sea. There, would, then, be an end of his mischief; but a false witness on behalf of Jesus

Christ is the most mischievous traitor on the face of the earth. He does more harm than a thousand false hostile witnesses against Him. Oh! my friends, to be *good* witnesses for Jesus Christ. The more a witness is supposed to know of the truth to which he testifies, the greater his responsibility. Oh! for a minister to be a bad witness, as some of the prophets of old were. Look at the awful things God says about them that lead His people into the ditch, caring more about the fleece than the sheep—awful! For a mother to be a bad witness in her family, and to take her little children, clinging on to her skirts, right to the edge of the pit! For a master to be a bad witness—to profess to be a Christian, and to be a bad witness before his men; for a Sunday school teacher to be a bad, inconsistent, false witness of Jesus Christ in his class; for members of Christian churches to be bad witnesses to one another, and to the world; who can tell the awful results? Oh! it is this inconsistent witnessing that has lowered and lowered the standard of practical Christianity till we have not got any standard left—till the landmarks are so obliterated, that there are not any to be seen.

FAITHFUL witnesses! He wants us to be faithful witnesses.

I want to note *one or two qualifications of a faithful witness,* and, oh, may the Holy Spirit help us.

The first qualification, then, of a faithful witness, is *A personal knowledge of the facts to which he witnesses.* If a witness in a court of justice begins to talk of what he thinks, feels, and believes, " Oh! hush, hush," says the judge, " we can't have that; we want to know what you KNOW—what you have seen, heard, and felt of this case;" and these are the sort of witnesses Jesus Christ wants, who can get up and say, "I KNOW!" The sort of witness that St. Paul was, who could look his judge in the face and say, "I would that thou wert altogether such as I am, save these bonds." What an impudent man he must have been, if he was not a sanctified man. What a supreme egotist! Those are the sort of witnesses. How Agrippa must have felt, just then. How the tables were turned. "Oh! I am turned into the dock, and here is the prisoner taking his seat upon the bench." That is the sort of witnessing we want. "I would that thou wert *altogether* such as I am, except these bonds." Could you stand up in the dock and say that? Could you stand up in your own house and say it? Could you stand up *anywhere* and say it? That is what the Lord Jesus Christ wants— people who know, who experience, who realize, who live the things they witness to. This is what the world is dying for—people who can get up and say, "I KNOW." The Lord wants people to tell the world they are saved. Can you? They will begin to listen to you then. You will begin to have some effect on them. They will begin to open their eyes and ears, and wonder whether it will be possible for God to save them. This is altogether different from a fine-spun theory *about* religion—this telling them that God has SAVED YOU. Not what we have learned in books. The world is sick of that. I don't wonder at intelligent men flying off from religion. I can make great excuse when I think what many of them have to listen to from Sunday to Sunday. As a gentleman

said to me, ' It's enough to sicken anybody. We do
get something in *The Times,* but, upon my word, I
can't keep awake at church. It is not that I would
not, if I could, but I can't.' Poor fellow! how I
pitied him.

No! not what is got from books ; not a dry, fine-
spun theory, from mere hearsay. When a witness
begins with what he heard someone say, ' Oh, hush !
says the judge, ' we don't want that, we want to
know what you have seen. Keep to the facts.' Jesus
Christ wants you to keep to the facts. Tell them, as
John says, what you have seen, and heard, and handled,
and realised of the truth of God. *Personal knowledge!*
It is wonderful how simple salvation language is,
when you have learnt it by experience and are
prepared to speak plainly to the people.

Then, a faithful witness must *tell the truth, and the
whole truth.* He must not hold back anything on
account of personal inconvenience, suffering, loss, or
gain, but must tell the whole truth. Oh! I tremble
to think what will be the fate of some who set
themselves up as teachers, and who have "kept back
part" of the truth because, to their apprehension, it
was not palatable or profitable to mankind. What
have I got to do with that ? I have to preach the
truth—the beautiful, whole. round, diamond, luminous
with Divine light, and not a base, muddy, paste
imitation, half truths manufactured into damning
errors, by which Satan is decoying thousands to Hell.
Give men the whole truth—both sides: the side that
relates to God ; and the side that relates to man ;
and be done with the nonsense of making God
contradict Himself, for " God is light, and in Him is

no darkness at all." If there were contradictions, there would be darkness. No; the darkness is in our own poor, blind, puny brains, and not in God or in His Book. In His Book, rightly interpreted, there is no contradiction whatsoever. The *whole* truth: the convicting truth as well as the healing truth; the sword as well as the balm; the running in of the Divine knife as well as the pouring in of the Divine oil. As Paul says, in the 26th chapter and 18th verse, "To open their eyes, and to turn them from darkness to light, and from the power of Satan unto God, that they may receive forgiveness of sins." He says he preached to the Jews and Gentiles that they should repent. This is the Apostle Paul, the great expounder of Justification by Faith, "That they should repent," and what?—oh, you legal Paul, what?— "Do works meet for repentance." Oh, Paul, I thought you were saved from works altogether, and had done with the Law. Oh! you preach works, and doing works meet for repentance. That is not Gospel, Paul! He significantly adds, "For this cause the Jews caught me, and tried to kill me:" and for that cause the Pharisees have been trying to kill God's true, whole-truth witnesses ever since, for they don't like the doctrine that cuts idols and sin in twain, and that says, "Bring forth fruits meet for repentance."

The faithful witness must give the whole truth; and he must give it personally, too A faithful witness must give it himself. He can't witness by proxy. He may pay one hundred and fifty evangelists to go and witness in his place: that is all right. It is no more than he ought to do—two hundred and fifty, if he has money enough—because the Master claims all that he has, little or much, every farthing of it, however many preachers he may send and maintain.

Therefore, he can never do any more than he ought, but that will not exonerate him from the personal obligation. God will say to him: If I have put my candle in you, it is that it may shine for somebody else's benefit. If I have given you the bread of life, it is for you to go and break it to the famishing multitudes round about you. YE are my witnesses. You may pay the minister and the missionary, but you must do it yourself, too, for how can *one* witness make up *for two?* True, God wants the minister to witness, and it is no more than his duty if he witnesses all day long as long as he lives. But that will never make up for your lack of service. YOU must witness ; and *there are some souls with whom you have more influence than any other living being*—some souls that you can better get at than any other person— some souls that, if you do not save, will, probably, never be saved at all. Ye are my witnesses, and, if ye have the grace and love and light of God, it is at the peril of your soul if you hide it.

Then, in the next place, *faithful witnesses must speak out, not mince the matter*—not " mumble," as they say in court. The judge makes the witness speak up so that everybody may hear him. *He must be heard.* " Speak out." And why should not the Lord's witnesses speak out ? I wonder when we shall be done with this sneaking, hole-and-corner, shame-faced religion ! I wonder when Christian England will cease to be ashamed of its God ! ! The only nation under Heaven ashamed of its religion and its God is the one

that has got the true God to worship and to love.
What an anomaly ; Speak out ! !

David knew nothing about this mincing, half-and-
half, milk-and-water sort of religion. David rejoiced
to tell of his righteousness before the great congregation. He was always telling about His goodness, and
His Law, and singing about it all the day long, dancing
before the ark sometimes, and doing all manner of
demonstrative things to glorify his God. And that
was not enough, for when he had called upon all
human kind to praise Him, he called on the hills and
the trees to clap their hands and to dance for joy.
We want some of *that* sort of religion nowadays.
Talk of the new dispensation, I wish we could get a bit
of the old one back.

The interests of truth demand this out-spokenness.
How is error to be met but by the bold proclamation
of the truth ? How are the emissaries of Satan
palming upon mankind his lies—always at it, night
and day—how are they to be silenced but by witnesses
faithfully crying in their ears, " This is a lie, and that
is a lie. This is the truth and this is the way ; we
know, we see, we feel—walk ye in it." Turn ye, turn
ye, for why will ye die ? They want out-spoken
witnesses. There are plenty of false witnesses now, as
there ever were, and what does Jesus Christ want?
He wants His true witnesses to come out and face
them, and be a match for them—not to sneak away in
holes and corners, and be ashamed of their religion,
and talk about an " unobtrusive religion "—unobtrusive
nonsense. There is no such thing ! Come out before
the world. As Elijah said, " If the Lord be God,
follow Him," serve Him, speak for Him ; " but if

Baal " be God, " then follow him." Then away with
all this nonsense, your sanctuaries, and Bibles, and
profession—have done with it all and follow Baal. Be
one thing or the other. Methinks there wants an
Elijah now to come and ring it through all England.
I would like to see any man get up and make a
straightforward recognition of, and appeal to, God in
our Houses of Parliament, and I would like to see how
he would be greeted.

I was thinking, as I was passing the Royal Exchange
and saw on the top, " The earth is the Lord's and the
fulness thereof," how many believed it who walked
beneath its shadow. I wonder what anyone would be
thought of, were he practically to recognise the fact.
' Oh ! ' they would say, ' he's not fit for his post—
you'll have to take him away ; he's a little affected in
his head.' Oh ! you know it is so ; but God is not
mocked, though men think He is. God sits in the
circle of Heaven, and though the people do rage, and
the heathen imagine a vain thing, and the kings of
the earth set themselves, He is laughing at them, and
by-and-bye will come their calamity.

We say the world is dying ; what for ? Sermons ?
No. Periodicals ? No. Religious stories ? Oh ! dear
no. There is no chance of a want of them for many
a long year to come. Dying for disquisitions ? No.
For fine-spun theories ? No. For creeds and faiths ?
Oh ! you might have them by the dozen. What is it
dying for ?—downright, straightforward, honest, loving,
earnest testimony about what God can DO FOR SOULS.
That is what it wants. That is what those poor men
in the shops, those walking up and down Oxford
Street, in the theatres, in the dancing saloons, in the

concert rooms, everywhere, that is what men want:
somebody to come and take them lovingly by the
collar, and tell them that GOD IS GOD, and that He
can save them 'He has saved me, my brothei, and
He can save you!' *That* is what the world wants.
One word like that is better than a sermon, and it will
do more for God and the salvation of the world. Oh,
yes, men are saying, in fact all over this land—
thousands, 'Here I am; I am a poor slave of sin. I
know it.' They say it in their consciences, though
they do not say it to you. They say it often to us
when they are pushed into a corner by the swoid of
the Spirit. 'I know I am wrong, sinful, wicked.' As
that dear John Allen, whose life I have been telling
about, said once when sitting swearing, surrounded by
his companions, and somebody said to him, 'Jock, if
you were to die, what would become of you?' 'I
should go to hell, straight!' He was an honest fellow.
He knew where he was going, and he said it.

I said to a gentleman, 'Mr. So-and-so, what about
your soul?' He said, 'It's in a devilish state.' Poor
man! He knew where he was going, and there are
thousands like him. Do you think they don't feel
their bondage? Have they not got a mind and a
conscience? Have they not a better side, as you call
it, to their nature? Has not God flashed the light of
His Holy Spirit upon their dark souls, and have they
not struggled and striven? Yes, but they say, 'There
is no health in us; there is no help foi us. We have
done making resolutions and trying to be better; we
cannot. There is no hope in us.' And there they aie
waiting for somebody to come and tell them there is
HELP IN GOD. They say, 'I see precious little

difference in you religious folks. I have never known
anybody that religion has seemed to do much for.'
And, when they are told to believe, they laugh at you,
and I don't wonder at it. The poor human conscience
is better instructed than many of its teachers. It
wants to be put RIGHT, and it says, Is there any hope?
Can God save such as I am? Has He saved anybody
like me from this thraldom, from this slavery, from this
misery, from this constantly going down in the mud?
Did He ever *save* anybody LIKE ME? And sometimes
he goes to chapel or church, and hopes the minister
will tell him, when lo, he begins a dissertation about
the resurrection, or the divinity of Christ, or something
the man has believed all his life, and so he is
disappointed again, and he says, ' This is of no use to
me.' Oh! friends, I speak the things I know from
testimony of scores of souls. In fact, I could not
repeat it, it would make your faces burn to hear what
men of intelligence, thought, and standing have said
to me in many an ante-room where I have been
labouring. It is time there was a change. The world
is famishing for lack of real spiritual bread. It wants
something to eat, and you give it a stone! but *God is
raising a people who know what it wants and how
to give it,* who know how to break the bread of life,
and testify what God has done for them, and what He
can do for other poor famishing souls ; who can go and
say : ' Here my friend, He can save such as you. I
was such a one once. I was a slave of sin, the slave
of drink, or a blasphemer, or a liar, or a thief, or
addicted to some bad secret habit worse than any of
these. I was such a slave, and He has saved me. He
has broken my fetters and set me free, and I am the

Lord's free-man. He has saved me and He can save you,' That is what the world wants—TESTIMONY WITNESSING.

Has He saved any of you? Are you testifying to your poor, famishing, sinking fellow-men? Do you ever look at them and think where they are going? Do you pity them, love them, long after them in the bowels of Jesus Christ? Do you know anything of that longing? If so, how can you forbear testifying? "Ye are my witnesses of these things," everywhere, at all times, amongst all people ! !

It is in the nature of the case that a *witness must witness before other people,* before living hearers. That is the place to witness, and before enemies, and when he does not know which way the wind will blow, or how the words of God will be received. He must be a true witness, even if he has to seal his testimony with his blood.

This was the kind of witnessing the martyrs did. I often wonder whether there would be any martyrs now. Sometimes I think that the greatest boon to the Church of Christ would be a time of persecution. I believe it would. I believe it would drive us up to God and each other. We should find out, then, whether we were willing to forsake all to follow Him. You know that if the martyrs had taken the standard of religious life that exists now, they would never have been martyrs. They would have looked after their own skins, and left the Lord to look after the Gospel. If they might have been allowed a little latitude, and gone halfway, there would not have been any martyrs, because they could nearly all have got off with that; but they felt it necessary to be faithful right through, and to stand by the whole truth to the very last jot and tittle, and when they could have got off by saying three words on a paper, they refused to do it, and went to the stake, and let the flames lick up their blood. Those are the witnesses the Lord wants —outside, everywhere, always at it. Always witnessing. 'Always,' you say. Yes; always. Why? *Because men are always dying and being damned!* If the Bible is true—everywhere—your friends and your neighbours around you. You get a letter: 'Oh! Mr. So-and-so is dead—only ill three days—thirty-six hours—twenty-four hours—gone!' Ah! and the echo in many a soul afterwards is, what would I give for a chance to go and have one talk with him. But he's gone—*somewhere!* Where is he gone? If he were unwashed and unpardoned and unsaved—where is he gone? I got so wrought up once upon this point that I thought I should have lost my reason. I could not sleep at night with thinking of the state of those who die unsaved. Dare I think about it? WHERE IS HE GONE? *Oh! it was this view of the case that led me to open my mouth first in public for God.*

I have promised some friends here to-night to give this illustration from my own experience, or else I rarely refer to it. I had long had a controversy on this question in my soul. In fact, from the time I was converted, the Spirit of God had constantly been urging me into paths of usefulness and labour, which seemed to me impossible. Perhaps some of you would hardly credit that I was one of the most timid and bashful disciples the Lord Jesus ever saved. For ten years of my Christian life my life was one daily battle with the cross—not because I wilfully rejected, as

many do, for that I never dared to do. Oh, no ! I
used to make up my mind I would, and resolve and
intend, and then, when the hour came, I used to fail
for want of courage. I need not have failed. I now
see how foolish I was, and how wrong ; but, for some
four or five months before I commenced speaking, the
controversy had been signally roused in my soul which
God had awakened years before, but, which, through
mistaken notions, fear, and timidity, I had allowed
almost to die out. I was brought to very severe
heart-searchings at this time. I had not been realising
so much of the Divine presence. I had lost a great
deal of the power and happiness I once enjoyed.
During a season of sickness, one day it seemed as if
the Lord revealed it all to me by His Spirit. I had
no vision, but a revelation to my mind. He seemed
to take me back to the time when I was fifteen and
sixteen, when I first gave my heart to Him. He
seemed to show me, all the bitter way, how this one
thing had been the fly in the pot of ointment, the
bitter in the cup, and prevented me from realising
what I should otherwise have done. I felt how it had
hindered the revelation of Himself to me, and hindered
me from growing in grace, and learning more of the
deep things of God. He showed it to me, and then I
remember prostrating myself upon my face before
Him, and I promised Him there in the sick room :
' Lord, if Thou wilt return unto me, as in the days of
old, and re-visit me with those urgings of Thy Spirit
which I used to have, I will obey, if I die in the
attempt. I care not ; I will obey.' However, the
Lord did not re-visit me immediately. He let me
recover, and I went out again. About three months

after that I went to the chapel of which my husband was a minister, and he had an extraordinary service. Even then he was ever trying something new to get the outside people. They were having a meeting in which ministers and friends in the town were taking part, and all giving their testimony and speaking for God. I was in the minister's pew, with my eldest boy, then four years old, and there were some thousand people present. I felt much more depressed than usual in spirit, and not expecting anything particular, but, as the testimonies went on, I felt the Spirit come upon me. You alone who have felt it know what it means. It cannot be described. I felt it to the extremities of my fingers and toes. It seemed as if a voice said to me, ' Now, if you were to go and testify, you know I would bless it to your own soul as well as to the souls of the people,' and I gasped again, and I said, in my soul, ' Yes, Lord, I believe Thou wouldst, · but I cannot do it.' I had forgotten my vow—it did not occur to me at all. All in a moment, after I had said that to the Lord I seemed to see the bedroom where I had lain, and to see myself as though I had been there prostrate before the Lord promising Him that, and then the voice seemed to say to me, ' Is this consistent with that promise ? ' and I almost jumped up and said, ' No, Lord, it is the old thing over again, but I cannot do it,' and I felt as though I would sooner die than do it. And then the Devil said, ' Besides, you are not prepared to speak. You will look like a fool, and have nothing to say.' He made a mistake. He overdid himself for once. It was that word settled it. I said, ' Ah ! this is just the point. I have never yet been willing to be a

10

fool for Christ, now I will be one;' and without
stopping another moment, I rose up in the seat, and
walked up the chapel.   My dear husband was
just going to conclude.   He thought something had
happened to me, and so did the people.   We had been
there two years, and they knew my timid, bashful
nature.   He stepped down to ask me 'What is the
matter, my dear.'   I said, 'I want to say a word,'   He
was so taken by surprise, he could only say, 'My dear
wife wants to say a word,' and sat down.   He had
been trying to persuade me to do it for ten years.
He and a lady in the church, only that very week,
had been trying to persuade me to go and address
a little cottage meeting, of some twenty working
people, but could not.   I got up—God only knows
how—and if any mortal ever did hang on the arm
of Omnipotence, I did.   I felt as if I were clinging
to some human arm—and yet it was a Divine arm—
to hold me.   I just got up and told the people how
it came about.   I confessed, as I think everybody
should, when they have been in the wrong and mis-
represented the religion of Jesus Christ.   I told the
people, although I had been occupying all the
ordinary positions of a minister's wife, though I was
young then, I had been doing a great deal more than
many an elderly one does in the Church of God, in
the way of meeting believers, and visiting and
working behind the scenes, so that they had all been
regarding me as a very devoted woman, and I told
them so.   I said 'I dare say many of you have been
looking upon me as a very devoted woman, and one
who has been living faithfully to God, but I have come
to know that I have been living in disobedience, and

to that extent I have brought darkness and leanness into my soul, but I promised the Lord three or four months ago, and I dare not disobey. I have come to tell you this, and to promise the Lord that I will be obedient to the Heavenly vision.'

But oh! how little I saw then what it involved. I never imagined the life of publicity it was going to lead me into, and of trial also ; for I was never allowed to have another quiet Sabbath, when I could speak or stand up. All I took there was the present step. I did not see in advance, but the Lord, as He always does, when His people are honest with Him, and obedient, opened the windows of Heaven, and poured out such a blessing, that there was not room to contain it.

There was more weeping, they said, in the chapel that day, than ever there had been before. Many dated a renewal in righteousness from that very moment, and began a life of devotion and consecration to God.

Now, I might have ' talked good ' to them till now, and that would never have happened. That honest confession, coming out and testifying the truth, did what twenty years talk would never have done.

The work went on. Whenever I spoke, the chapel used to be crowded to its utmost capacity, and numbers were converted. Not to me but to God be all the glory. Shame to me that I did not begin sooner. It was not I that did this, but the Holy Ghost, the Holy Spirit of God.

The Lord dealt with me in a very wonderful way. Three months after this, my dear husband fell sick for the first time, and he was obliged to go away into the country. A deputation waited on me, to ask me to take his town appointments. I said I could not think of such a thing. What could I do with that great congregation? They must not ask me—and away they went. They came back again to know if I would take the nights, they implored and importuned me until I promised. So you see, God forced me to begin to think and work. I was obliged, and I did it with four little children, the eldest then four years and three months old. It looked an inopportune time, did it not, to begin to preach? It looked as though the Lord must have made a mistake. However, He gave me grace and strength, and enabled me to do it; and while I was nursing my baby, many a time I was thinking of what I was going to say next Sunday, and between times noted down with a pencil the thoughts as they struck me. And then I would appear sometimes, with an outline scratched in pencil, trusting in the Lord to give me the power of His Holy Spirit; and I think I can say that from that day —and it is about nineteen years and nine months since —He has never allowed me to open my mouth without giving me signs of His presence and blessing. Don't you see that while the Devil kept me silent, he kept me comparatively fruitless; now I have ground to hope and expect to meet hundreds in Glory, whom God has made me instrumental in saving. The Lord dealt very tenderly with me : giving me great encouragement, but some things were dreadful to me at first. I would not go into pulpits till the people demanded it. And the first time I saw my name on a wall!—I shall never forget the sensation. Then my dear husband said, ' When you gave yourself to the Lord, did you not give

Him your name?' Thus he used to go fiom one thing to another, until now I have learned to glory in the Cross. When a dear friend was talking, the other day, about the tremendous undertaking it was to go to France and begin there ; I said, ' My dear sir, I should not feel any more discomposed to go to France, and open there next Sunday, than I should to appear in St. Andrew's Hall, simply for this reason, that I believe God is the same in every place, and the same faith, and the same truths and the same faithfulness will bring Him to our help.' " Ye are my witnesses," saith the Lord, " And, lo, I am with you ALWAYS ! "

Will you be encouraged, my sister ? Never mind trembling. I trembled. Never mind your heart beating. Mine beat nearly through. Never mind how weak you are. I have gone many a time from the bed to the pulpit, and back from the pulpit to bed. It is not by human power, wisdom, might, or strength—it is by my Spirit, saith the Lord. He loves to use the weak things, that the excellency may be seen to be of God. If your neighbours were sick of some devastating plague, and you could go and help them, would not you do it ? Would you say, ' I am only a woman, and I cannot ?' ' Oh,' you would say, ' let me go, like Miss Nightingale did to the sick and wounded soldiers. Let me go.' And these are not the bodies, but the *souls.* They are dying. They are going to an eternal death. Will you not rise up ? Oh ! suppose all the Christians in this hall to-night were to begin, from this hour, to be faithful, and consistently testifying everywhere for Jesus, what a commotion there would be ! How many, think you, would be converted in a month's time ? How would they begin flocking like doves to the windows? How would the ministers, some of them, begin to wake up? The people would go and beseech them morning, noon, and night. God wants you to witness right out everywhere, in the darkest courts and alleys and in Oxford Street alike. Begin, and the Spirit · ·of God will fall upon you, and however they may try to get rid of the Holy Ghost, they will not be able to do it when God has got hold of them. We catch thousands of people in this way who never intended to be converted. Every day I live, the more I am convinced that if God's people were to be in desperate earnest, thousands would be won; but they are not likely to be won by the genteel fashion of putting the truth before them—so common nowadays—because nobody thinks they are in any danger! If you believe it, *begin.* The Apostle says you are to be good, valiant soldiers of Jesus Christ: the old Christians were all this; they fought a good warfare, and they overcame the Devil by the "blood of the Lamb and the *word of their testimony.*" Be soldiers for the Lord, and He will give the victory, and you shall go and take prisoners. Great big giants, black-hearted infidels, black-hearted blasphemers, they shall go down before you like little children, because the Lord of Hosts will put His Spirit in you. "Ye are My witnesses." Witness! WITNESS!! of Me everywhere and always. The Lord help you. Amen.

FILLED WITH THE SPIRIT.

FILLED WITH THE SPIRIT.

ACTS i 4.—"*And being assembled together with them, commanded them that they should not depart from Jerusalem, but wait for the promise of the Father.*"

EPHESIANS v. 18 —"*Be filled with the Spirit.*"

I THOUGHT, perhaps, it would meet a difficulty of some who are present this afternoon, to state, with respect to last Sabbath's address, that this exhortation to be filled with the Spirit is given broadly to all believers. If my remarks, at that time, conveyed the idea to anyone, that there were merely a privileged few who are called to be thus filled with the Spirit—to be, as it were, the leaders of the rest, and others were to abide, and must abide, on a lower platform of Christian experience, I certainly did not intend them to do so. God forbid that I should insinuate anything of the kind, because I do not believe it. I believe that this injunction is given broadly to all believers everywhere, and in all times, and it is as much the privilege of the youngest and weakest believer here to be filled with the Spirit, as it is of the most advanced, if the believer will comply with the conditions, and conform to the injunctions of the Saviour, on which He has promised this gift. I do not find two standards of Christian experience here at all. I do not believe God ever intended there should be a lower life and a higher life, and I am afraid that those people who rest in the lower life will find themselves awfully mistaken at last. I believe that religion is all or nothing. God is either first or He is nowhere with us, individually. The very essence and core of religion is, " God first," and allegiance and obedience to Him first.

If I cannot keep my father and mother and be faithful to God, then I must forsake my father and mother. If I cannot keep my husband or wife, and be faithful to Him, then I must forsake husband or wife. If I cannot keep my children and be faithful to Him, then, Jesus Christ says, forsake them. And if I cannot keep my houses and lands and be faithful to Him, then I must forsake them. If I cannot keep my business and be faithful to Him, then I must sacrifice my business, and if I cannot keep my health and be faithful to Him, then I must sacrifice it, and, last of all, if I cannot keep my life and be faithful to Him, then I must be prepared to lose it, and lay my neck on the block, if need be. That is my religion, and I do not know any other. I do not believe any other will stand on the right hand of the throne; and, if that be so, why, all other sorts must stand on the left. If this be not true, I am utterly and thoroughly mistaken in the first principles of Christianity, and I will come and sit down at anybody's feet who can convince me that I am wrong. So, pray, do not attach that idea to me that I think that any person can sit down, providing he has light, or with opportunities of getting light, without embracing this higher-life religion, and then get into Heaven in this shame-faced, sneaking way. No, no!—God will have you, or He will not have you. He will know you, or will say, " Depart from Me, I know you not." The Lord help you every one.

This Pentecost is offered to all believers. It comes, or it would come, in the experience of every believer, if he would have it. God wants you to have it. God calls you to it. Jesus Christ has bought it for you, and you may have it and live in its power as much as these apostles did, if you will—every one of you. My dear friends, you may have it, be filled with it, and no one but God knows what He would do with you, and what He would make of you if you were thus filled, for the experience of Peter shows you how utterly different a man is *before* he gets a Pentecostal baptism and *after* he gets it. The man who could not stand the questionings of a servant-maid before he got this power, dared to be crucified after he got it. I may just say, that here is the great cause of the decline of so many who begin well. Oh! there is no more common lament on the lips of really spiritual teachers, everywhere, than this, that so many begin well. "Ye did run well." we might truly say of thousands in this land to-day, "Ye did run well." They begin in the Spirit, and then, as the Apostle says, "They go on to be made perfect by the flesh." How is this? Because, you see, the Spirit puts before every soul this walk of full consecration and whole-hearted devotedness to God, and, instead of being obedient to the heavenly vision, the soul shrinks back and says, 'That is too much—that is too close—that is too great a sacrifice,' and they decline, and, instead of giving up a profession and going back into the world (there would be ten times more hope of them if they did that) they cling on to the profession and kindle a fire of their own, and walk in the sparks they have kindled. But He says He is against them, and "they

shall lie down in sorrow." Oh! there is a deal of this.
People must have a God and a religion. They will
have one, and when they shrink from the true one,
and will not follow the Divine counsel, then they
make one for themselves, and a great many of them
go to sleep and never wake again. They go out of
the world comfortably under the influence of narcotics,
and they never wake. They die deceived; or, if they
do awake, we know what sort of an awakening it is,
and what sort of deathbed theirs is. Our poor
Salvation Army people—these "fishermen,"—these
young women—are sent for to pray with these people
when they get awakened. And oh! what scenes are
witnessed. Oh! see to it that you get awake and
keep awake, and be willing to follow the Spirit's
teaching, in everything, at all costs and sacrifices.

I want you to note, first, how these people waited.
"Tarry at Jerusalem till ye be endued with POWER."
Mark, that is not truth merely. They had got truth
before. There is something besides truth needed.
Paul says his Gospel and his preaching were not
merely in word, but in *power*, and in the demonstration
of the Spirit. What would be the first thing that
would strike you that these disciples would be thinking
of, as they wended their way back from Olivet, having
taken leave of their now glorified Master? Back
again to the upper room at Jerusalem. Imagine what
state of mind would be theirs. How would they wait
for the promise?

Methinks the first feeling would be that of deep
self-abasement. As they thought of the past; now
that the full glory of His Divinity, and the Divinity
of His mission had burst upon them, and, as they

thought of their three years' sojourn with Him, and of all their darkness and blindness of heart, and all they had lost—all that they might have known—all He would have revealed to them, if they would have received it—as the thought of it all burst upon them —just as, next day, when you find out who a person was, or some particular circumstance respecting a person that you did not fully understand at the time, and, when the person is gone, and it all breaks upon you, you say, ' What a fool I was,' and so methinks these apostles would say. Indeed, as He said, " Oh, fools, and slow of heart to believe ! " They were cured —Peter certainly was—of self-sufficiency, of pride, and all of them would go back again in deep self-abasement.

Can you not think you see them, as they assembled in the upper room ? I should not be surprised at all if Peter, with his impulsive nature—and it is a glorious thing to have an impulsive nature when it is impulsive for good—to be zealously affected always in a good cause—threw himself on his face before his risen Master in deepest humiliation and broken-heartedness for his base ingratitude in having denied Him. And how do you think Thomas and all of them would feel as they remembered the scene in the Garden, and how they all in the hour of His agony, forsook Him and fled ? How would they all feel ? Oh! they would feel indeed unholy, untrue, cowards, and would go down, over and over again, on their faces, to wait in deep self-abasement.

And now, friends, this is the very first and indispensable condition of receiving the Holy Ghost. You must first realize your past impurity, unholiness, disobedience, and ingratitude. You must not be afraid to know the worst of yourselves. You must look back at the time when your hand has been with Him on the table, and yet you have virtually betrayed Him. You must look at your unfaithfulness and disobedience, at your shrinking from the cross, at your cleaving to the world, and if you want to be filled with the Spirit, you must be willing to know the worst of yourself, and tell the Lord the worst of yourself. You must say, 'Now, Lord, am I low enough? Now, Lord, am I down far enough in the dust for Thee to come and lift me up? I abhor myself. I loathe myself in dust and ashes, and I want Thee to come and fill me with Thy Spirit.' You will have to be emptied of self. When people are self-sufficient, God always leaves them alone to prove their self-sufficiency. When people think they can do for themselves, He lets them fall down and see their weakness. We must realize our utter helplessness and weakness—we must be utterly lost in our own sight. Some of you, I think, have come to that, and others are not quite low enough. You must get down lower, my brother. God's way to exaltation is through the Valley of Humiliation. You must get lower—lower. You can never get too low in your own estimation in order to be filled with the Spirit of God. They waited, secondly, in earnest appreciation of its importance. Ah! they had enough to make them do it. How do you think they felt when they got into the upper room? We are told that there were about 120 of them. How do you think they felt as they thought of the past, remembered the ignominious crucifixion of their Lord, looked forward to the future, and contemplated the work to which

He had called them? And what was it? It was not to go and set up an idol of Jesus Christ alongside of other idols in the temples of heathen gods, but it was to go into the city of Jerusalem, where they had just crucified Him between two thieves, and proclaim Him as the long-expected Messiah of the Jews. It was to begin to set up the Royal Spiritual Kingdom in contradistinction to their temporal and earthly kingdom, and then to go out from Jerusalem and subjugate the world to His sway! How would they feel? Poor Peter, and Thomas, and John, and Mary and the rest of the women (thanks to the Holy Ghost, He has taken care to put it in that they were there)—how would they feel? They would feel, 'We might as well stop and die here, as go out as we are, until we do get the equipment of power. We want something more than we have got.' And there they waited, and they said, 'Lord, pour it out upon us; we are ready. We are helpless, we are powerless—we can do nothing. Thou knowest what Thou hast called us to do, and Thou hast promised this power to perform it. Now, here we are. It is useless for us to begin until we get power.' They appreciated its importance. God never gave this gift to any human soul who had not come to the point that he would sell all he had to get it. Oh! it is the most precious gift He has to give in earth or in Heaven—to be filled with the Spirit, filled with Himself (as we said last Sunday), taken possession of by God; moved, inspired, energised, empowered by God, by the great indwelling Spirit moving through all our faculties, and energising our whole being for Him. That is the greatest and most glorious gift He has. He is not likely to give it to people who do not highly appreciate it, and so highly that they are willing to forego all other gifts for it—everything else, creature love, creature comfort, ease, enjoyment, and aggrandisement for this one thing. Have you come to that? Are you telling the Lord so? Are you sincere? If you are really sincere in what some of you write me, then some of you have come to it;—but, oh, how people can deceive themselves. My heart has been awfully pained during this last week with one or two instances of this kind that have come to my notice. I have been half the week, I think, with Elijah under the juniper tree. I have cried, "Lord, who hath believed our report?" Who will thus take hold of God for this special and full salvation? Alas! how few. One draws back for one reason, and another for another. One feels how far they come with us. You can hear the tread of their feet, and you can hear how they falter and draw back. None but those who travail for souls can ever understand the agony of feeling that souls are drawing back when you have brought them on the road so far. I have thought many a time of the Saviour, when so many who had been hearing Him forsook Him and fled. It was after He had been trying to lead them higher, even to real spiritual union with Himself.

They were not willing to go all the way—to pay all the price—to suffer all the consequences—but, if you want this blessing, I know no other way. I had to come to this before I got it. The last idol of my soul had to be renounced, and it was hard work, as it always is, because we *love idols.* Idols would not be idols if they were not beloved. But we have to lay our real

Isaac, our beloved and only Isaac, upon the altar. It is hard work, but it has to be done, because He is a jealous God, and will have no rivals. Do you so appreciate this blessing that you are willing to give up your Isaac? If so, you may have it this afternoon. He will fill you with His Spirit.

Third, and lastly, they waited *in obedient faith.* How do we know? Because *they did as He bid them* —that is the evidence. He said, "Go, tarry in the city of Jerusalem." Peter might have said, when he had seen his Lord off to Heaven, 'Well, what am I going to do now? I have been a long time running after the Lord in Palestine, I must betake myself to the fishing. I can wait as well on the sea beach as in Jerusalem. I wonder why the Lord told me to go to Jerusalem? I think it was rather unreasonable. He might have thought of my old father and mother at home. I think I shall go back to my fishing-nets.' No, no, they had been cured of their unbelief by the last few days' experience. They had learned better than to dictate to their Master, and they knew He had a good purpose in sending them to Jerusalem, and so they went there and did as He bade them— straight. Back to that upper room they went. Mary might have said, ' I have been running about ministering to the Saviour a long time, I'm afraid my friends will think I am neglecting home duties and the claims of old friends. I really must go home and see to matters a bit; I may as well wait there for the Holy Ghost as at Jerusalem.' No, Mary had learned better. She went back to Jerusalem. We have got their names. And they entered into the

11

upper room, and shut the door, and waited—
obedient faith ! One of your poets said—

> " Obedient faith that waits on Thee,
> Thou never wilt reprove."

No, it is the disobedient faith that is sent empty
away. Oh ! people are crying out about their faith,
but it is their disobedient faith. If the Lord has told
you to wait in any particular place, or way, or
company, or time, and you disobey Him, you will
never get it, and you will have to come to those
conditions at last, even if it is on your dying bed !
Obedient faith ! While there is a spark of in-
subordination, or rebellion, or dictation, you will
never get it. Truly submissive and obedient souls
only enter *this* kingdom. Anywhere He tells you to
go, anything He tells you to sacrifice, or fly from,
you will have to do. This is one of His choice gifts
that He has reserved for His choice servants, those
who serve Him with *all their hearts.*—Obedient faith !

But you say, ' How do you know it was faith ?' Oh,
because we know they did as He bade them. Now,
faith is inseparable from expectation. Where there is
real faith there is always expectation, and when I hear
people praying, as I often do, *from their throats,* for
the Holy Ghost, and see how they talk the minute
they get up from their knees, and know how they live
and whom they associate with, and how they spend
their time, I say, ' Yes, you may pray till your dying
day, but you will never get it.' If they expected
anything, they would wait for it : common sense tells
us that.

Those people waited. How long? What a hue and
cry there is now about us Salvation Army people

spending whole nights in prayer. People—Christians, grey-headed Christians, up and down the country—say to me, 'I don't know how you get the time over. It must be such an immensely long time. Do you really mean to say that you spend all night in prayer?' I say, 'Yes, with just an interval for putting the truth and showing the people how to apply it to their own consciences.' Then they say, 'It must seem an awfully long time.' I suppose it does, to them, to spend one whole night in prayer; but here, we are told, they waited ten days, till the Day of Pentecost was fully come. I have no doubt they went as far into the night as they could keep their natural powers awake. They waited. They did not set the Lord a time. They were wiser. They did not say, 'Now we will go and have a couple of days of it. That will be a long time. We will just shut out all else and wait on the Lord for a couple of days, and if He does not come by that time, it will be outrageous to wait beyond it. Whoever heard of a prayer-meeting two days and two nights' long?' They did not set the Lord a time! They went and waited till it came.

You say, "No; I have not got it." No; because you did not wait until it came. You got hungry, or you fell asleep, or hugged your idol. You did not wait TILL IT CAME.

Suppose they had given up on the fifth day and said, 'There must be some mistake. He knows we are here, all ready, and the world is perishing for our message. There must be some mistake. We had better begin.' But no, they waited on, and on, and on, until it came. Can you imagine what sort of prayers went up from the upper room? Do you think they

were the lazy, lackadaisical, prayers that we hear every
now and then for the Holy Spirit ?

Oh ! how would Peter agonise and wrestle : how
would Thomas plead ; how would Mary weep, beseech,
and entreat, and how were they all of one heart and of
one accord. They wanted the one thing, and they
were there to get it. They cared for nothing else but
that. They cried for it as hungry children cry for
bread. *They wanted Him* Did the Lord ever disappoint
anybody who waited like that ? Can anybody say so
here ? Did you ever hear of such a case ? Never.
HE CAME.

Oh ! but there are some people, nowadays, who set
God times in everything. They think a good deal
more about their dinners than about Him. They
think a great deal more about intercourse with their
friends and doing the polite to them, than they do
about the precious waiting Holy Spirit of God. They
think a great deal more about their businesses. ' Oh! '
they say, ' it is business, and business must be attended
to.' But what about the Holy Ghost and the Kingdom ? Must not the Kingdom of God be attended to ?
Must not your soul be saved, and must you not become
a temple of the indwelling Spirit of God ? Put a MUST
in there, if you please. Far more important is the
soul than the body. Friends, are these things so, or
am I only imagining them ? Are these great truths,
or are they fables ? These are the most common-
sense, simple exhibitions and illustrations of these
truths that could possibly be given. Was it not so ?
Did they not thus wait, and did not the Holy Ghost
come ?—and when He came *He sat upon each of them.*
Bless His name.

People have a wonderful habit of losing sight of the little words of the Bible—the people who make a great to-do about the Word in other ways, often say 'I never saw that till you directed my attention to it.' Suppose I were to say that this afternoon something happened to each person, would you imagine I meant the men, and not the women ? Of course you would say, I meant everyone. And it filled them all—the women as well as the men, and they began to speak with other tongues, as the Spirit gave them utterance. *He came.*

And, my friends, He comes yet. My bodily senses have been quite cognisant of His coming sometimes. We only know that we feel something that so influences our bodies that we cannot describe it.

In the North, when I was there, we had an all-night of prayer, at which one thousand people, admitted by ticket, waited all night on God. The meeting began at ten, and went on until six in the morning, and there were strong men, men in middle life, and old men, lying on their faces on the floor. There were doctors there, who examined them and tried to account for it from physical causes, but they could not. *It was the power of God.* The Holy Ghost *does* come, and because, in coming thus into our souls, and thus filling us, He sometimes prostrates our bodies, people rebel, as they did on this occasion, and reject the manifestation, and say, ' Excitement! fanaticism ! ' What right have you to say that the Holy Spirit coming into a human soul can operate upon that soul to the full extent without, to some degree, prostrating the body ? We know how people fall under great emotions of anger, grief, and joy. Why ? Because

the influence of the mind has so affected the body
that the body cannot bear it, and when the Holy
Spirit of God comes into a human soul and opens its
eyes, and quickens its perceptions, and enlarges its
capacity, and swells it with glory, is it an unlikely or
improbable thing that the body should sometimes be
prostrated under His power? What did Paul say?—
" I bear in my body the marks of the Lord Jesus,"
and I have been into " the third heaven and heard
unspeakable words which it is not lawful to utter."
Do you think God intended such experiences and
visions only for Paul and the Apostles? Ah! there
have been many since his day who have had such
experiences, and many more of God's people *might*
have them, if they would, but they are not willing to
be wrapped in His arms; they are not willing to be
pressed to His bosom; they are not willing to know
Him in the Scriptural sense; they are not willing to
be given up and consumed by His Spirit. Their heart
and flesh do not cry out after the living God, as
David's did. They are not panting after Him as the
hart after the water-brooks. They are not longing to
come and appear before God. If they were so longing
that they could not live without it, then God would
come and be revealed to them. Will you, then, wait
in obedient faith?

Oh! I have the most awful realisation that you will
be eternally better or worse for these services, and so
I want you to come up higher, I don't want you to go
back, and get cold and indifferent to these things,
because here is the hope of the world, if there is any
hope for it, in people getting filled with the Spirit,
people getting so woke up to God and His glory, and

the interests of His kingdom, that they should be just as anxious for souls as other people are for sovereigns. Filled with the Spirit, having eyes to see spiritual sights which others do not see, ears to hear the crying of the famishing multitudes who are dying for lack of knowledge; hearts to feel so that they could go and weep over them. Hands to break the bread of life; and, if need be, a zeal that will lead them to die for them. This is what we want, and it only comes with the fulness of the Spirit.

Are you willing, my brother? are you willing, my sister? If so, stop with us this afternoon. Never mind the dinner; never mind the tea. You have taken care of the outer man long enough, now look after the inner man. Never mind the children, mother, just now, the Lord will take care of them. Never mind anything, you who are athirst, but, getting this blessed Holy Spirit of God, this full baptism of it on your souls. The Lord help you. Amen!

THE WORLD'S NEED.

THE WORLD'S NEED.

MATTHEW xxi. 23.—" *Son, go work to-day in my vineyard."*

LUKE xiv. 23.—*" And the lord said unto the servant, Go out into the highways and hedges and compel* them *to come in, that my house may be filled."*

WE might have enumerated other texts, teaching the same truths. There are plenty of them, but the general tenor and bearing of the Word of God, especially of the New Testament, is more significant than even direct and isolated texts. It seems to me that no one can disinterestedly and dispassionately study the New Testament without arriving at the conclusion that it is a fundamental principle, under-lying the whole, that His light and grace is expansive; that is, God has, in no case, given His light, His truth, and His grace to any individual soul, without holding that soul responsible for communi-cating that light and grace to others. Real Christianity is, in its very nature and essence, aggressive. We get this principle fully exhibited and illustrated in the Parables of Jesus Christ. If you will study them, you will find that He has not given us anything to be used merely for ourselves, but that we hold and possess every talent which He has committed to us for the good of others, and for the salvation of man. If I understand it, I say this is a fundamental principle of the New Testament.

How wonderfully this principle was exhibited in

the lives of the Apostles and early Christians! How utterly careless they seemed to be of everything compared with this—this was the first thing with them everywhere! How Paul, at the very threshold, counted nothing else of any consequence, but willingly, cheerfully gave up every other consideration to live for this; and how he speaks of other Apostles and helpers in the Gospel who had been nigh unto death, and laid down their necks for the work's sake; and we know how he travelled, worked, prayed, wept, and suffered, bled and died, for this one end. And so with the early Christians, who were scattered through the persecutions, how they went everywhere preaching the Word; how earnest and zealous they were, even after the Apostolic age, we learn from ecclesiastical history—how they would push themselves in everywhere; how they made converts, and won real, self-denying, followers even in king's courts; how they would not be kept out, and could not be put down, and could not be hindered or silenced. "These Christians are everywhere," said one of their bitterest persecutors. Yes, they were instant in season and out of season; they won men and women on every hand, to the vexation and annoyance of those who hated them. Like their Master, they could not be hid; they could not be repressed; so aggressive, so constraining, was the spirit which inspired and urged them on.

It becomes a greater puzzle every day to me, coming in contact with individual souls, how people read their Bibles! They do not seem to understand what they read. Well might a Philip or an angel come to them and say, "Understandest thou what

thou readest?" Oh! friends, study your New
Testament on this question, and you will be alarmed
to find to what an awful extent you are your brother's
keeper—to what an awful and alarming extent God
holds you responsible for the salvation of those
around you.

I want to glance, FIRST, at *our call to work for God;*
and, SECONDLY, at *two or three indispensable qualifications for successful labour.*

And, *first,* as I have just said, we are called by
the Word not only in these direct passages, but by
the underlying *principle* running through it all, and
laying upon us the *obligation to save men.* In fact,
the world is cast upon us : we are the *only people
who* CAN *save the unconverted.*

Oh! I wish I could get this thought thoroughly
into your minds. It has been, perhaps, one of the
most potent, with respect to any little service I have
rendered in the vineyard,—the thought, that Jesus
Christ has nobody else to represent Him here but us
Christians—His real people : nobody else to work for
Him. These poor people of the world, who are in
darkness and ignorance, have nobody else to show
them the way of mercy. If we do not go to them
with loving earnestness and determination to rescue
them from the grasp of the great enemy; if we do
not, by the power of the Holy Ghost, bind the strong
man and take his goods, who is to do it? God has
devolved it upon us. I say this is an alarming and
awful consideration.

Secondly, we are called by the Spirit. The very
first aspiration, as I said the other night, of a newly-
born soul is after some other soul. The very first

utterance, after the first burst of praise to God for deliverance from the bondage of sin and death, is a prayer gasped to the throne for some other soul still in darkness. And is not this the legitimate fruit of the Spirit? Is not this what we should expect? I take any one here, who has been truly saved, to record if the first gushings of his soul, after his own deliverance, was not for somebody else—father, mother, child, brother, sister, friend? Oh! yes, some of you could not go to sleep until you had written to a distant relative, and poured out your soul in anxious longings for his salvation;—you could not take your necessary food until you had spoken or written to somebody in whose soul you were deeply interested. The Spirit began at once to urge you to seek for souls; and so it is frequently the last cry of the Spirit in the believer's soul before it leaves the body. You have sat beside many a dying saint, and what has been the last prayer? Has it been anything about self, money, family, circumstances? Oh! those things are now all left behind, and the last expressed anxiety has been for some prodigal soul outside the kingdom of God. When the light of eternity comes streaming upon the soul, and its eyes get wide open to the value of souls, it neither hears nor sees anything else! It goes out of time into eternity, praying as the Redeemer did, for the souls it is leaving behind. This is the first and last utterance of the Spirit in the believer's soul on earth; and oh! if Christians were only true to the promptings of this blessed Spirit, it would be the prevailing impulse, the first desire and effort all the way through life. It is not God's fault that it is not so. In personal dealing with souls there is no point comes out more frequently than this : nothing which those who have really been converted and have become backsliders in heart more frequently confess and bemoan than their unfaithfulness to the monitions of the Spirit with respect to other souls. In fact, backsliding begins here in thousands of instances. Satan gets people to yield to considerations of ease, propriety, being out of season, being injudicious, and so on ; and they lose opportunities of dealing with souls, and so the Spirit is grieved and grieved. Oh ! what numbers of people have confessed this to me.

A gentleman, in advanced life, said : 'When I was a young man, and in my first love, the zeal of the Lord's house so consumed me that I used to neglect my daily business, and could scarcely sleep at night ; but, alas! 'that was many years ago.' 'Was it not better with you *then* than *now?'* I asked ; and the tears came welling up into his eyes. Oh, yes! the Lord says of him, "I remember thee, the kindness of thy youth, the love of thine espousals, when thou wentest after me in the wilderness, in a land that was not sown ; Israel was holiness unto the Lord, and the first-fruits of His increase." And, Alas! there are many such to-day. They have it all to do over again ; they have to repent and do their first-works ; they have to come back and get forgiven, and washed, and saved, if they are to go into the kingdom on high, all for want of systematically and resolutely obeying the urgings of the Holy Spirit towards their fellow-men.

Now, you have, some of you, been hearing, the last few Sundays, about grieving the Spirit, and about being filled with the Spirit ; and some of you are puzzled as to how you ought to wait—whether you ought to go on with your lawful avocations and wait. I say: My friends, I could quite justify the position I took up last Sunday, but I will not stop, for I do not care about circumstantials; but mind, *this* is the great point—you must so wait, wherever it may be—so plead, and wrestle, and believe—SO THAT YOU GET IT. Then I care not whether it be in Jerusalem, in the Upper Room, or anywhere else—*only, get it.* Don't let us lose the substance in quibbling about the way. Wait in that way congenial to your present circumstances; but, oh! wait for it until you get it, for this is the life of your souls, and the life of many souls, perchance, besides yours. You want this *spirit*—the spirit that yearns over the souls of your fellow-men; to weep over them as you look at them in their sin, and folly, and misery; the spirit that cannot be satisfied with your own enjoyments or with feeling that *you* are safe, or even that your children are safe; but that yearns over every living soul while there is one left unsaved, and can never rest satisfied until it is brought into the kingdom.

Such are the urgings of the Spirit; and if people would only be obedient to them, they would never lose these urgings. Why, what an anomaly it is! Does it look reasonable, or like God's dealings, that people should begin so strong, like the old man felt when he was young, and, instead of waxing stronger, and having this holy zeal and desire *increased*, get weaker and weaker, and less and less? Does it look like God's way of doing things? Oh, no! This eclipse is through grieving and quenching the Spirit.

Now, my friend, you are called by the Spirit to this

woik. Obey the call—DO IT. Nevei mind if it chokes
you—do it. Say, "I had better die in obedience than
live in disobedience." Oh! these everlasting likes and
dislikes. ' I don't like to speak to that person,' ' I so
dislike wiiting that letter.' "Oh! you don't know what
might be the consequences." Never mind the
consequences—do it. God will stand between you and
consequences; and, if He lets you suffer, never mind—
then suffer; but obey the voice of the Spirit. There
would have been thousands of souls saved if all those
who have had these urgings had obeyed them. Pray,
where do these urgings come from? Do they come
fiom your own evil hearts? Then you aie better than
the Apostle. Sepaiated from the Spirit that dwells in
you, and disunited fiom Chiist, your living Head, you
aie selfish, *devilish.* Then where do these urgings
come from? Do they come fiom the Devil? Satan,
then would indeed be divided against himself. Where
do they come from? It is the Spirit of the living God
that is uiging you to come out and seek to save the
lost. Will you obey these urgings? Will you give
up your reasonings? Will you give up your likes and
dislikes, and OBEY? If you will, then He will come to
you more and more, till, like David, you will feel the
interests of His kingdom to be more to you than meat
or drink, than silver or gold. Nay, you will become
like him who said, "The zeal of Thine house hath
eaten me up."

But, further, *we are called to this work by what He
has done for us.* And what is that? Oh! you say, I
cannot tell. No, no; we shall have to get *home* fiist,
and then we shall never be able to tell. We shall
never be able to cast up *that* sum, not even for the

12

gratification of the angels. That will remain an unexplored quantity for ever, what He has done for us!! We shall have to find out what it would have been to have been lost! and what it is to be saved in all its fulness and eternity, before we can tell what He has done for us!!

What has He done for us? Oh! if we had a tithe of the love to sinners that He had for us, of His forbearing patience, of His persevering effort, when He followed us day and night, reasoned and reasoned with us, wooed and allured us, what could we not do?

I remember reading, somewhere, the story of a nobleman who was (I think) a backslider. He was stopping at some country inn, and he went up into a room in which, over the mantelpiece there was a very good picture of the crucifixion by a good old master, and under it was written, "I suffered this for thee— what hast thou done for Me?" This question went home. It struck deep. He thought—Yes, what indeed? He went out into the stables to his horses, to try to get rid of the uncomfortable impression, but he could not forget it. A soft, pathetic voice seemed to follow him,—'I suffered this for thee—what hast thou done for Me!' At last it broke him down, and he went to his knees. He said: 'True, Lord, I have never done anything for Thee, but now I give myself and my all to Thee, to be used up in Thy service.'

And have you never heard that voice in your soul, as you have been kneeling at the Cross? Did you ever gaze upon that illustrious sufferer, and hear His voice, as you looked back into the paltry past? What hast thou done for Me?

Now, there have been, at the least, something like

350 people, who have come forward, so far, in these
services, professing to give themselves afresh and fully
to Jesus. I am sure, in the main, they have been
sincere. They have come for the witness of the Spirit
to their adoption, and for power for service. Now,
friends, I want to know what this is to come to—what
is to be the end of it ?

> " What are you going to do, brother ?
> What are you going to do ? "

And sister, too. Is it going to die out in sentiment ?
Is it going to evaporate in sighs and wishings, and end
in ' I CANNOT ? ' God forbid ! What are you GOING TO
DO ? What HAVE you been doing for Him the last
week ? Ask yourselves. You say—' Well, I have read
my Bible more.' Very good, so far as it goes. What
have you read it for ? ' Well,' you say, ' to get to know
the Lord's will, and to get instruction and comfort.'
Aye, exactly, but that is all for *yourself*, you see. ' I
have prayed a great deal.' Very good. I wish everybody would pray. The Apostles say all men everywhere
ought to pray. What for ? ' I have been asking the
Lord for great things.' Very good, praise the Lord ;
but those are for yourself, mainly. If you have been
led out in agonising supplication for souls, thank God
for it, and go on, as the Apostle says, "watching
thereunto, with all perseverance," "praying in the Holy
Ghost ; " but if it has been merely praying to get all
you can for yourself, what profit is that to the Lord ?
But you say—' I am bringing up my family.' Exactly;
so are the worldly people around you, but what for ?
For God or for yourself ? Oh ! let us look at these
things, friends. I am afraid a great deal of the religion
is a mere transition of the selfishness of the human

heart from the world to religion. I am afraid a great
deal of the religion of this day ends in getting all you
can and doing as little as you can—like some of your
servants. You know the sort, who will do no more
than they are forced—just get through, because they
are hired. There is a great deal of that kind of service
in these days, both towards man and towards God.

Now, friends, what have you been doing for HIM—
for the promotion of *His* blessed, glorious, saving
purposes in the world? What have you been denying
yourself for the sake of His kingdom? What labour
have you gone through of mind, or brain, or heart?
How many letters have you written? How many people
have you spoken to? How many visits have you made?
What self-denying labour have you been doing for Him
who has done (as you say) so much for you? What
have you been suffering for Him? Have you been
trying, in some little measure, to fill up behind the
measure of His sufferings "for His body's sake, the
church?" Have you been carrying the sins and sorrows
of a guilty world on your heart before God, and pleading
with Him for His own name's sake, to pour out His
Spirit upon the ungodly multitudes outside, and to
quicken half-asleep professors inside? Have you been
subjecting yourself to reproach and contempt—not
only from the world, but from half-hearted professors
and Pharisees, bearing the Cross, enduring the shame
of unkind reproaches in living and striving to save
them? Oh, what have you been doing, brother and
sister?

Come, now, friends, I want a practical result. He
suffered that for you. He is up yonder, interceding
for you. Five bleeding wounds He always bears in

the presence of His Father for you. If He were
to forget you for a single moment, or cease His
intercession, what would happen? What are you
doing for Him? He has left you an example that
you should follow His steps. What were they?
They were blood-tracked; they were humiliated
steps. They were steps scorned by the world. He
was ignored, and traduced, and rejected of men. He
had not where to lay His head. He carried in His
body and in His soul the sorrows and sufferings of all
our race. He was a man of sorrows—not His own.
He had no reason to be sorrowful. He was the
Father's own beloved, and He knew it, but He was a
man of sorrows, and acquainted with grief. The
griefs of this poor, lost, half-damned world He bore,
and they were sometimes so intolerable that they
squeezed the blood out of His veins. Have you
been following in His footsteps, in any measure?
He lived not for Himself. He came not to be
ministered unto, but to minister, and took upon Him
the form of a servant. What are you doing? Oh!
my friends, up, up, and be doing. Begin, if you
have not begun—begin to-day. Ask Him to baptise
you with His Spirit, and let you begin at once to
follow Him in the regeneration of the Spirit. You
are called by what He did for you!

Then, you are called by the wants of the world. I
have said so much about this at other times that I
will not say more now, only methinks it is a theme
that is never exhausted, and never will be while
there are any more sinners to save. Oh! the wants
of the world! To me it is an overwhelming, a
prodigious thought, that He shed His blood for every

soul of man, and that, as He hung there, He saw,
under all the vileness, and sin, and ruin of the Fall
—the human soul created originally in His own
image, and capable of infinite and eternal develop-
ment and progress. The soul to be rescued, washed,
redeemed, saved, sanctified, and glorified—He saw
this glorious jewel, and He gave HIMSELF for it.
Look at these souls.   There is not one of them so
mean, or vile, or base, but can be rescued by the
power of His Spirit, and by His living, glorious Gospel
brought to bear upon them.   The Saviour, quoting
from the Prophets, says, " Ye are gods (and adds) the
Scriptures cannot be broken." He had no such little,
mean, insignificant estimate of the worth of human
souls, as some people have nowadays, who consign
whole generations to hell without any bowels of mercy
or compassion.   Oh! the Lord fill us with the pity
of Jesus Christ, who, when He saw the multitudes,
wept over them.

Oh! friends, think of one such soul! What is your
gold, or houses, or lands—what your respectability,
what your reputation, what all the prizes of this
world? We talk about it, but who realises it—*who,
who?*—the value of one precious, immortal soul
saved, redeemed, sanctified?   Oh, the wants of the
world! They are dying, THEY ARE DYING!! When
people come to me with their fastidious objections, I
say—" My friend, all I know is—souls are dying,
dying."

If your homes were being decimated by the cholera,
you would not be very particular about the means you
used to stay it, and if anybody came with objections
to the roughness of your measures, you would say,

'the people are dying, they are dying,' and that would
be the end of all argument. I say, they are dying,
and they ARE to be saved. Satan is getting them:
I want God to have them. Jesus Christ has bought
them. He was the propitiation for the sins of the
whole world. They belong to Him, and He shall have
everyone I can reach, and everyone I can inspire
others to reach also.

The world is dying. Do you believe it? You are
called by the wants of the world. Begin nearest home
if you like, by all means, I have little faith in those
people's ministrations who go abroad after others, while
their own are perishing at their firesides. Begin at
home, but do not end there. "Oh! yes," people say,
"begin at home," but they end there; you never hear
of them anywhere else, and it comes to very little what
they do at home, after all. God has ordained that the
two shall go together. Get them saved by all means,
but get somebody else saved as well. Set yourself to
work for God. Go to Him to ask Him how to do it.
Go to Him for the equipment of power and then begin.
Never mind how you tremble. I dare say your
trembling will do more good than if you were ever so
brave. Never mind the tears. I wish Christians
would *weep* the Gospel into people; it would often go
deeper than it does. Never mind if you do stammer.
They will believe you when it comes from the heart.
They will say, 'He talked to me quite natural,' as a
man said, some time ago—wondering that he should
be talked to about religion in a natural way; but mind,
no mock feeling, for they will detect it in a minute.
Go to the closet until you get filled with the Spirit,
and then go and let it out upon them. Finney says

"I went and let my heart out on the people." Get your heart full of the living water and then open the gates and let it flow out. Look them in the face and take hold of them lovingly by the hand and say, 'My friend, you are dying, you are going to everlasting death. If nobody has ever told you till now—I have come to tell you. My friend, you have a precious soul. Is it saved?' They can understand that! not beginning in a roundabout way, but talking to them straight:—'Do you ever think about your precious soul? Is it saved? Are your sins pardoned? Are you ready to die?' Your rich neighbours and your servant-girls and your stable-men alike, can understand that.

A lady said to my daughter, 'I have begun talking to people about their souls in quite a different way to what I used. I begin asking them if they do not know they are sinners and if ready to die, and it produces quite a different effect.' For one reason she has her own heart full of the Love and Spirit of God, and that burns her words in. Begin in that way and see what God will do through you, for, of course, I only recognise you as the instrumentality which He has chosen, and those who reflect upon the instrumentality reflect upon His wisdom. You go and put your hand to the plough and He will give you strength to push it along.

The Lord help you to go home thinking about the wants of the world, and next Sabbath we will consider the qualifications for labour.

THE HOLY GHOST.

THE HOLY GHOST.

LUKE xxiv. 49.—*" And, behold, I send the promise of My Father upon you : but tarry ye in the city of Jerusalem, until ye be endued with power from on high."*
ACTS i. 8.—*" But ye shall receive power, after that the Holy Ghost is come upon you."*

FRIENDS who were present at former services will remember our line of thought, without my stopping to recapitulate. My chief reason for taking up this subject again, after having preached four sermons on it, is to meet the difficulties of some whom I believe to be anxious and honest enquirers. Taking those who have written and spoken to me as representatives of a class, it occurred to me that there might be many others in a similar state of mind, and it is a great joy to me if the Lord uses me to meet real difficulties, and to help those who are exercised by them into a higher state of grace, and a more thorough and complete devotion to the Lord. This is my end—God is my witness—in every service.

Now, I do not want to make any reflections, and will not do so any further than I can help ; but in dealing with such a subject we cannot avoid this, to a certain extent, as I have said before ; if the truth reveals error, and if trying to get into a better track necessarily in some measure reflects on the old track— we cannot help it, and we must not eschew the former for the atter. It must be manifest, I think, to every spiritua. nd thoughtful Christian that there is a great want somewhere in connection with the preaching of the Gospel, and the instrumentalities of the church at large. That there are many blessed exceptions I joyfully and gladly admit. No one hails them with greater gladness than I do. That there are blessed green spots here and there in the wilderness is quite true, and when these are gathered together and descanted on in articles, they look very nice, and we are apt to take the flattering unction to our souls that things are not so bad after all ; but, when we come to travel the country over and find how few and far between these green spots are, and hear what a tide of lamentation and mourning reaches us all round the land as to the deadness, coldness, and dearth of Christian churches, we cannot help feeling that there is a GREAT WANT SOMEWHERE ! This is not only my opinion, but it is almost universally admitted, that, with the enormous expenditure of means, the great amount of human effort, the multiplication of instrumentalities during the past century, there has not been a *corresponding result.*

People say to me, on every hand, we have meetings without number, services, societies, conventions, conferences, but what comes of them all, *comparatively?* And I may just say here that numbers of ministers and clergymen, in private conversation, admit the same thing. In fact, none are more ready to admit this comparative lack of results than many dear spiritual ministers. They say, when talking with us behind the scenes—' Yes, it is a sad fact. I think I preach the truth. I pray about it. I am anxious for results, but alas ! alas ! the conversions are but few and far between.' And then, not only are those con-

versions few, but in the mass of instances superficial—
we should expect from such a putting of the truth as
that we have been reading about, numerous and
continual turnings to the Lord as in those days—we
should expect men coming out openly from sin and
from God-dishonouring courses, businesses, and professions—coming out from fashionable and worldly
circles, abjuring the world, and literally and absolutely
following the Christ as in those days. That is what
we have a right to expect, and yet how comparatively
rare they are, so that when people do this, there is
quite a commotion, and it is talked about all over
the land Now I say this is universally admitted,
and it behoves us to ask before God and with an
earnest heart-yearning, desiring to improve this state
of things. *Where is the lack, what is the want ?*

Now note, secondly, this want is not the truth. Oh!
what a great deal of talk we have about the truth, and
not any too much. I would not yield to any man or
woman in this audience in my love for this Bible. I
love this Word and regard it as the standard of all
faith and practice, and our guide to live by ; but it is
not enough of itself. *The great want* is not the truth,
for you see facts would contradict this theory. If it were
the truth, then there would be no lack at this day,
compared with other times, because we never had so
much of the truth. There never was so much
preaching of the truth, or such a wide dissemination
of the Word of God, yet, comparatively, where are the
results ?

Further, not only as to *quantity,* but as to
quality am I discouraged. Not only are there
comparatively few conversions, but a great many of

these are of a questionable kind. We should not only ask—are people converted, but what are they converted to? What SORT OF SAINTS ARE THEY? Because, I contend, you had far better let a man alone in sin than give him a sham conversion, and make him believe he is a Christian when he is nothing of the kind. So you see we must look after the quality as well as the quantity, and I fear, we have an awful amount of spurious production, and it behoves us—and I will, for one, if I were to be crucified for it to-morrow—be true to what the Spirit of God has taught me on this point, I will never pander to things as they are for fear of the persecution which follows trying to put them right. God forbid!

Then, I say, the lack is not *truth*. There will be thousands of sermons preached to-day—the truth, and nothing but the truth. Nobody will pretend to say they were not in perfect keeping with the Word of God; and yet they will be perfect failures, and nobody will know it better than they who preach them! *These are facts.*

I was talking, on this point, a while ago, with a good man, who said, ' Ah! yes, I have not seen a conversion in my church for these two years' Now, what was the reason? There *was* a reason, and I am afraid many might say the same. Yet there are the unconverted They come to be operated upon. Take a church where there is a congregation of, say 800 or 1,000, suppose with a membership of 200 or 300. What becomes of the 500 or 700 unbelievers, who come and go, Sunday after Sunday, like a door on its hinges, neither the better nor worse?—nay, God grant it might be so, but they are worse. They get enough light to light them down to damnation, but they do not get enough power to lift them into salvation. *What* IS THE MATTER? There must be something wrong. Will you account for it. It ought to be accounted for! It ought not so to be. God is not changed. Surely He is as anxious for the salvation of men now as He ever was. Human hearts are not changed; they are neither better nor worse; they are depraved, vile, devilish—just the same. The Gospel is exactly the same power it ever was, rightly experienced, lived, and preached. It is still the power of God unto salvation. Then what is the matter? The truth is preached. The people hear it, and yet they remain as they were. Where is the lack?

Now, I say, and I most unhesitatingly assert, that the great want is POWER—this power of which we have been reading.

And I want to remark, thirdly, *that this power is as distinct, and definite, and separate, a gift of God, as was this Book, as was the Son, or any other gift which He has given us*

It is distinctly recognised, not only in our texts, but, as we read to you again and again, as a distinct and definite gift accompanying the efforts of those who live on the conditions on which God can give it to them. We cannot explain this gift, but it is the power of the Holy Spirit of God in the soul of the speaker accompanying His word, making it cut and pierce to the dividing asunder soul and spirit. " You shall receive *power* after that the Holy Ghost is come upon you." " Until you be endued with,"—not the truth, not faith (they had faith before that), but,— " power; " and, as He says in another place, " I will give you a mouth and wisdom, which all your adversaries shall not be able to gainsay nor resist." Though they may stone you, as they did Stephen, they shall be cut to the heart, and made to feel the power of your testimony.

Now, I find people who go to work, which is all right, because the power comes to us in obedient faith; but they go trusting in their own efforts. They are without this endowment of power, and they see no result. The work is a comparative failure. Oh! what numbers of people have come to me who have been at work in different directions, in churches, as ministers, elders, deacons, leaders, Sabbath-school teachers, tract distributors, and the like, confessing that they had been working for more or less lengthened periods, and had seen comparatively little result. They say, ' Do you think this is right? Do you think I ought to go on?' Go on, assuredly, but not in the same track. Go on, most decidedly, but seek a fresh inspiration. There is something wrong, or you would have seen some fruit of your labour—not all the fruit. God does not give to any of us to see it all; but we do see enough to assure us that the Holy Ghost is accompanying our testimony. God's people have always done that when they have worked in conformity with the conditions on which the power can be given.

Now, this is how I account for the want of results— the want of the direct, pungent, enlightening, convicting, restoring, transforming power of the Holy Ghost; and I care not how gigantic the intellect of the agent, or how equipped from the school of human learning, I would rather have a Hallelujah Lass, a little child, with the power of the Holy Ghost, hardly able to put two

sentences of the Queen's English together, to come to
help, bless, and benefit my soul, than I would have the
most learned divine in the kingdom without it, for it is
"not by might, nor by power, but by My Spirit," Oh!
that you would learn it. When you have learnt that,
you will be *made*· when you *experience* it, you will lay
hold on God. It is not by might, any kind of might
—might of intellect, or learning, or eloquence, or
position, or influence; it is not by might, nor by power
—man's power—of any sort, but by My Spirit. That
is as true as it ever was. HERE IS THE SECRET OF THE
CHURCH'S FAILURE! She is like Israel of old. She
hath multiplied her defenced cities and her palaces, but
she hath forgotten the God of Israel, in whom her
strength is. If you will read the history of the church
from the beginning you will find that true which I say,
that just to the degree that the church has increased
in the material she has decreased in the spiritual. I do
not say it ought to be so; I do not say that is a necessity.
I only give you a significant fact that *it has been so.*

You say—'How do you account for it?' I account
for it because we poor, wretched, tiny, helpless creatures,
although we cannot get anything good in the creature,
yet put some TRUST in it. But when God teaches us that
we have nothing to trust in, when He makes us realise
our own nothingness and utter helplessness, and gives
us hold of Him with the grasp of despair, then we will
begin to be of some use—and *never till then.* It is
God worketh in us and by us. The Apostle labours all
the way through to show and convince everybody that
it was God in him and not of himself at all. Though
he *could* have preached with enticing words of man's
wisdom, and, no doubt, had many a temptation to do

13

it, as everbody has who has dipped into the flowery paths of human rhetoric and learning, yet he eschewed this as he would the Devil. He said, no!—"this one thing I do"—putting aside absolutely all else, he went on straight to that work, till they cut his head off.

I believe you *do* perceive; but, if you do not, take the Book and examine it yourself. Be at the trouble. You will not get at the mind of the Lord without a great deal of trouble on these matters of power, spiritual union, and the like. Take the Bible with you on your knees before the Lord; show Him the words, and say, 'Now, Lord, show me the meaning of this.' Wait, and there will come a voice from the excellent glory. There will come light as from the Shekinah, which will reveal it in your spiritual consciousness, and you will thus know that thing for ever. You will be wiser than your teachers with respect to that particular point.

Further, you say, 'Can we have this power equally with the early disciples?' I say, reasoning by analogy, assuming that what God has done in the past He will continue to do in the future, is it not likely that He will give it to us, because we equally need it?—we poor things, in our day, as they did in theirs, we equally need it : *first, because the character of the agents is the same.* We are very much like them, and they were very much like us. Thank God. It has often encouraged me. If they had been men of gigantic intellects and extraordinary education, training, and position; if they had possessed all human equipment and qualifications, we might have looked back through the ages in despair, and said, 'I can never be such as they were.' Look what they

were, naturally, apart from this gift of power. The
Holy Ghost has taken care to give us their true
characters. They were men of like passions, weak-
nesses, tendencies, liability to fall, with ourselves—
just such poor, frail, weak, easily-tripped-up creatures,
and, in many instances, unbelieving and disobedient,
before Pentecost. Now, I say this is encouraging
for us all.

You remember what Jesus said to Mary—" Go and
tell my disciples AND PETER." Mary, perhaps, would
have left Peter out after his shameful denial of the
Lord; for fear of this, Jesus said, " Go and tell my
disciples AND PETER."

Ah! there are some here saying, 'But Peter was
not so bad as I am.' Well, we don't know anything
about that, but, whether you are worse or not, the
Holy Ghost is equal to the emergency. He can cure
you. He can baptise you with His power. You may
have denied Him, if not as Peter did, yet practically
as badly. It makes no difference to God whether you
have been a little bad or very bad; whether you have
denied Him once or thrice, or whether you have
denied Him with oaths and curses. If you will only
come *and comply with the conditions,* He will look
on you, heal you, and baptise you with power. Did
they not all forsake Him and flee, except a few poor
faithful women? All the world forsook Him and fled
in the hour of His extremity. 'Ah!' you say, 'well,
I have done the same myself. I would not watch
with Him one hour. I have betrayed Him before
my friends and acquaintances in the world, where I
have been brought into circumstances that have tested
my fidelity. My courage has failed, and I have

failed to witness for Him.' Yes, I know and agree
with you that it was base ingratitude. You were a
traitor, indeed, but still, if you will come back, 'Peter,'
and repent, and do your first works, He will receive
you—baptise you with power. Oh! what they were
before Pentecost, and what they were after! Poor
Peter, who could not stand the questionings of a
servant maid, who could not dare to have it said that
he was one of the despised Nazarenes, what a
valiant soldier he afterwards became for the Lord
Jesus Christ, and how tradition says he was crucified
for his Master at the last. Anyway, we know he was
a faithful and valiant soldier to the end of his journey.

Now, this baptism will transform you as it did
them; it will make you all prophets and prophetesses,
according to your measure.

Will you come and let Him baptise you? Will
you learn, once and for ever, that it is not a question
of human *merit, strength or deserving at all*, but
simply a question of *submission, obedience, faith.*

Then we need it because not only are the agents
the same, *but our work is essentially the same.*

It may differ in its outward manifestations because
we live in an age of greater toleration, but it is just
the same in essence, and I do not know, as to the
manifestation, when you come to do it in Apostolic
fashion, with the Apostolic spirit, whether you do not
get very much the same Apostolic treatment. They
gnash upon you with their teeth, and do as much as
the law will let them, and sometimes a little more, in
the way of stoning and persecuting you.

The great thing to be done by this power of God
is to subdue the naturally evil, wicked, and rebellious

heart of man. Now God alone is able to do that
That is a superhuman work. You may enlighten a
man's intellect, civilise his manners, reform his habits,
make him a respectable, honest, industrious member
of society, without the power of God, but you cannot
transform HIS SOUL. That is too much for any human
reformer. That is the prerogative of the Holy Ghost,
and I have not a shadow of a doubt that the eternal
day will reveal every other kind of work to be wood,
hay, stubble. All the sham conversions, all the people
whose lives and opinions have been changed by anything short of this power will be wood, hay, stubble.
It is the prerogative of the Spirit of God. Therefore,
God never pretends to do it by any other means ; and
all the way through the Bible this power is ascribed
to the Spirit of God. Therefore, we want this Spirit
to do this work. What ! you set yourself to enlighten
a darkened human soul, to convince a hardened,
rebellious sinner, to convert a rebel in arms against
God, with an inveterate hatred in the very core of his
soul against God and all about God. You set yourself to bring down *that*—to transform that evil,
wicked heart, to subdue that soul to submission and
obedience !—you try it, try it without the Spirit of
God. Oh ! no, you want that Spirit. You want the
same measure of that Spirit, just the same, which
Paul had.

    And what is our work ? To go and subjugate the
world to Jesus ; everybody we can reach, everybody
we can influence, and bring them to the feet of Jesus,
and make them realise that He is their lawful King
and lawgiver ; that the Devil is a usurper, and that
they are to come and serve Christ all the days of

ARE IN NEED OF

their lives. Dare any of us think of it without this
equipment of power? Talk about 'Can we have it?'
—we are of no use without it. What can we do
without it? This is the reason of the effeteness of
so much professed Christianity; there is no Holy
Ghost in it. It is all rotten. It is like a very pretty
corpse—you cannot say there is this wanting or the
other wanting; it is a perfect form, but *dead*. It is
like a good galvanic battery. It is all right—perfect
in all its parts—but when you touch it there is no
effect—there is no fire or shock. What is the matter?
It only wants the fire—the power.

Oh! friends, we want the power that we may be
able to go and stretch ourselves upon the dead in
trespasses and sins, and breathe into him the breath
of spiritual life. We want to be able to go and touch
his eyes that he may see, and speak to the dead and
deaf with the voice of God and make them hear.
This is what we want—POWER

If we equally need it, *is it likely that God will
withhold it?* Why, the Book, rightly read and
understood, is full of promise and exhortation to get
it. Is it likely that if we are as frail as they were,
if the work is the same, is it likely that the God of
all grace, and our Father as much as theirs, and as
much in sympathy with the souls of men, will withhold it from us No, No. But our Saviour distinctly
told us that He bought it for us—that it was more
expedient that His people should have it than that
He should remain with them. It is promised to all
believers to the end of time. The conditions you
know—simply putting away everything that hinders,
casting aside every doubtful thing, trampling it in

the dust ; then a full, whole-hearted surrender to Him, embracing the Cross, embracing His will at all costs and sacrifices, and then a determined march to the upper room at Jerusalem and a determined abiding there until you get it—these are the conditions. Anybody can have it on these terms.

Then, in conclusion, let me remind you—and it makes my own soul almost reel when I think of it —that God holds us responsible. He holds you responsible for all the good you might do if you had it. Do not deceive yourself. He will have the *five* talents with their increase. He will not have an excuse for *one*, and you will not dare to go up to the throne, and say, 'Thou wast a hard Master, reaping where Thou hast not sown, and gathering where Thou hadst not strewn. Thou badest me to save souls when Thou knewest I had not the power.' What will He say to you ? 'Wicked and slothful servant, out of thine own mouth will I judge thee. You knew where you could have got the power. You knew the conditions. You might have had it. Where are the souls you might have saved ? Where are the children that I would have given you ? Where is the fruit ?' Oh ! friends, these are solemn and awful realities. If I did not believe them I should not stand here Oh, what you might do ! Who can tell ? Who would ever have thought, twenty years ago, when I first raised my voice, a feeble, trembling woman, one of the most timid and bashful the Lord ever saved, the hundreds of precious souls that would be given me ? I only refer to myself because I know my own case better than that of another ; but, let me ask you— supposing I had held back and been disobedient to

the Heavenly vision, what would God have said to me
for the loss of all this fruit? Thank God, much of it is
already gathered into heaven, people who have sent me
word from their dying beds, that they blessed God they
had ever heard my voice, saying that they should wait
for me on the other side, prepared to lead me to the
throne—what would have become of the fruit? *I*
should not have had it, anyway. They would never
have become *my* crown of rejoicing in the day of the
Lord. Oh, who can tell what God can do by any man
or woman, however timid, however faint, if only fully
given up to Him. My brother, He holds you responsible. He holds you responsible, my sister—you,
who wrote me about your difficulties and temptations
in testifying of Jesus—He holds you responsible.
What are you going to do? Ask yourself. It is
coming. You believe it. You say you do. Unless
you are a confirmed hypocrite, you do believe—that
you are going to stand before the throne of His glory.
You believe you are going to stand before Him by-
and-bye, when you shall receive according to the
things you have done in your body. What shall you
say? The world is dying—souls are being damned
at an awful rate every day. Men are running to
destruction. Torrents of iniquity are rolling down
our streets and through our world. God is almost
tired of the cry of our sins and iniquities going up
into His ears. What are you going to do, brother?
What are you going to do? Will you set to work?
Will you get this power? Will you put away everything that hinders? Will you have it at all costs?

We had a letter only on Friday, about a gentleman
who had been reconverted in the services of The

Salvation Army, telling us that he has relinquished an income of £800 a year, in order to keep a conscience void of offence—this is the result of the power of the Holy Ghost. I heard of another gentleman who was invited to a party. After dinner, the card-table was got out, as usual, and when the cards were all spread and everbody was ready to begin, this gentleman jumped up, and pushed it away, and said, ' I have done with this for ever.' The lady who told me said, ' He was down on his knees before we had time to turn round, and was praying for us and for all the house. 'Oh!' she added, ' you should have seen them.' Yes, of course, every man felt like the people round the Saviour. Every man's own conscience condemned him, ' They went off home, without any more card-playing, or dancing, or wine-drinking that night.' Come out from amongst the ungodly. Testify against them. Reprove them. Entreat them with tears. But be determined to deliver your soul of their blood. God will give you the power, and He holds you responsible for doing this—you people who have been coming here —who have received the light. WILL YOU DO IT ? If you will, we shall meet again, and rejoice with joy unspeakable. If you do, we shall praise God for ever that He brought us inside the walls of this building, long after it has mouldered into dust. There shall be children and grandchildren, and great grandchildren from you spiritually, if you will only be faithful.

1718740R0012

Printed in Great Britain
by Amazon.co.uk, Ltd.,
Marston Gate.